FRENCH LESSONS

*Best Wishes for a happy holiday season
& a prosperous New Year.*

Joseph C. French, Jr.

I hope you enjoy the book.

Joseph C. French Jr.

FRENCH LESSONS

Letters to My Daughters

Combray House

Cover design by Chloe French

ISBN: 978-0-578-64994-8

for my wife, Maureen Casey,
whose support makes everything possible

Contents

Foreword

Not a Rap Star

When I told my three daughters that I was writing a book, I tried to imagine what each of them might have been thinking. Their dad, an author?! Truth be told, there were many moments when I had a hard time believing this myself. In a long and challenging career, I have always striven to face adversity with a smile, viewing it as an opportunity. Even as a boy, I was so perennially optimistic that my mother once had me evaluated, as if happiness were a dangerous condition. Today, I work at Marcus & Millichap—this country's largest commercial real estate brokerage firm, where I am an advisor for institutional investment in real estate. But nothing in my career has tested my optimistic m.o. quite like putting pen to paper, or should I say voice to recorder, as much of what is written here began as something spoken.

I gave myself a difficult assignment. Inspired by the imminence of my middle daughter Eliza's wedding—*my baby is moving on*—I realized the time had come to share how I have made my way in worlds where I wasn't always welcome. But to do so, and in the positive spirit with which I have always striven to live my life, has meant detailing the intricacies and importance of a business that most people in our country take for granted, even as they may occasionally make potshots at it. The fact that my oldest daughter, Kate, is following in my business footsteps is a special source of paternal pride, reminding me also to stay on my proverbial toes and let nothing I say go unchallenged or unexplained.

Life has been my teacher in an education that has had many aha moments. I figured out when I was young that everyone can't be the president, nor do you have to be a rap star or some other kind of celebrity to be successful. I think of this especially when I follow the news, with so much of its cliched emphasis on fame and fortune. Of course we all want a roof over our heads, food on the table, and recognition by others of our contribution to community and country. But I sensed long ago that there has to be more to a rewarding career than the money you earn. Everything I have learned since has reconfirmed for me that the greatest joy is the gift of ourselves we can give to others. The hard part is deciding how.

The key for me has always been to understand both my shortcomings and strengths and then to figure out how to use my skills in something I want to do. Sounds easy, but I know better. I also know that while success in life, like business, is a choice, living a good life is not only possible while achieving that success but actually intrinsic to such accomplishment. But the last thing anyone else needs is another Business 101 book. So, I decided early on that I was going to write something different, a book like the one I wish someone had given me when I was a young man, before I discovered a world that as a boy I did not know existed. Think of what follows, then, as a life story of lessons and thanks for untold blessings that have come my way, none greater than my three, precious daughters, to whom this book is addressed.

Chapter 1

The Only One in the Room

December 27, 2017

Dear Kate, Eliza, and Chloe,

As the holidays come to a close, commemorating the end of another year, I find my thoughts focused on the future—of our country, its people and their wellbeing…and our family. What a change the new year will bring, with Eliza's wedding in Florence, Italy, next September! I hope it is a beautiful day and that everything she has worked on happens as planned.

Eliza, your nuptial represents a major change in my life. Another man will now share your life as you move onto this new stage in yours. Will you still ask me for financial advice and discuss life decisions with me?

As this event of great happiness looms ever larger, the prospect of these changes prompt me to reflect. I am reminded of the search that defines life for each of us. For me, this journey has invariably taken the form of a solution to a problem: how to live a life that enables me to support those I love, while contributing to the wellbeing of those with whom I work and others, less fortunate, whom I may not even personally know.

You may have noticed that I'm not one to hang award plaques in my office. Let your ego pump you up and next thing you know you fall off a curb. I could boast to others about my business, but as the proverb says, pride cometh before the fall. Life, as I've learned and relearned more times than I can count, has a way of happening, good and bad alike. But nothing simply evolves out of a mysterious ether, which brings me to what I will call French Lesson Number One: *You Make Your Own Life.*

To go back to the beginning of mine: while I was born in the Bronx, I spent most of my childhood on an estate in New Canaan, Connecticut, where your grandfather was the caretaker. I have little recollection of that first home in the Bronx, but I remember well the feeling of being my parents' only child until my brother came along when I was six years old. By then, we had left the Bronx and were ensconced in a cottage-like space built over the three-car garage at 691 Smith Ridge Road in New Canaan.

The estate was owned by W. R. Adams, president, CEO, and later chairman of the now defunct Saint Regis Paper Company. My father, Joseph French Sr.—everyone called him Frenchy—and my mother, Persephone, split their familial duties in a fairly traditional way that was typical of the times. Especially during the warmer months when there was much outside work to do, my dad was heavily invested in his job. Meanwhile, my mom, who was a trained nurse, oversaw my activities, making sure I got to school on time, taking me to my music lessons—I played the piano, beginning a lifelong love of music—and making certain I was properly dressed and well fed.

The day would come when my mother was concerned about my nonstop happiness and had me tested. She didn't understand, in a way that only later would I be able to explain, my discovery of avoiding stress in daily life: don't depend on others for your security. Today, when one of the sales people in my group come to me for help closing a deal, there is often an urgency in their request: they *need* this deal to close, whereas I *want* it to…but my world won't end if it doesn't. The advantage this gives me in negotiations of my own is huge.

Even after my brother Jacob's birth, I felt a special relationship with my mother. Her temperament could be volatile, triggering at one point a period when she left my dad, taking me with her, and moved back to the Bronx. A reconciliation soon followed. I was too young to understand the complexities of my parents' relationship, but that early awareness of its fragility prepared me for calamites that would come later. More profoundly, I was forced to begin forging a belief in my independence, to see and accept the reality that I was responsible for myself.

My father had been an athlete, and I inherited that gene. The New Canaan estate was so large—over 20 acres—that I even had my own baseball field, where I played pickup games with the three children from the Adams family. My father built a skating rink on the property, and when it froze in the winter we'd play ice hockey. Entering high school, I was only five feet, six inches tall and weighed just 106 pounds, so I knew I had to skate faster than the other players—that way they'd miss when they tried to check me. To get in better shape, when I wasn't skating I ran wind sprints.

My father worked dawn to dusk from March to November. Not until all the autumn leaves were collected and burned did he slow down for a few months. And my mother worked nights so she could be home to get my brother and me ready for school and be there when we came home.

As a boy, I took the bus to Center School for grades one through five. I was a good math student but had difficulty reading and writing because I was dyslexic, a condition that initially went undiagnosed, often leaving me in classes labeled remedial. When I think of all that now, it scares me to imagine the consequences of labelling or stereotyping people and groups in our country. Thousands of children at this very moment are being tested and diagnosed for so-called conditions that may define who they are their entire lifetimes. Workers are boxed into duties for which someone has concluded they are qualified, often with little hope of breaking the bond these jobs entail. And then

there is the pernicious and long-standing categoriza-
tion of people by race, gender, religion and age.

We've had many conversations, you three and I,
about the challenges of life that such
stereotyping creates. Each of you have dealt differently
with them. I remember when at the age of three Kate
asked me while we were in the grocery line why my
skin was darker than hers. Kate, my first born, you really put me on the spot then as everyone else in the
grocery line listened in. My answer was that wherever
in the world your family came from set the tone of
your skin. Dark skinned people originated in hot,
sunny paces, while light-skinned folks typically came
form parts of the world where the sun was not as
strong.

French Lesson Number Two: *Judge Not By Appearances*. May your lives present many opportunities
to refute the prospect and impact of such prejudice,
overt and insidious. Always believe in yourselves and
remember that knowledge of who you are is power.

But I'm getting ahead of myself…not for the
first time, nor I'm sure the last.

~

January 8, 2018

Seen through the prism of the present—here I am, still going to the office in White Plains each day, where I oversee my team of salespeople in the business of institutional property advisers; happily married to your mother Maureen, my best friend; in good health, no longer skiing or playing tennis but a regular presence on the golf course or Bikram yoga studio—seen, as I was starting to say, from my perspective today, it is tempting to romanticize my past. And I do think of myself as lucky. But whenever I remember New Canaan, I am reminded also of how it ended, not for me but for your grandparents, whose long, slow decline began when the man who would have been your Uncle Jacob was in college.

Jacob—who was always called Jay—and was named in honor of your great grandfather.

We did not share a bedroom. When my mother was pregnant with Jacob, Mr. Adams added two rooms to our place, so both my brother and I had our own bedrooms. Do you remember the story I told all three of

FRENCH LESSONS

you about the time our cousin Ronnie challenged us to
climb in and out of a

window in his house? Turned out there was a wasp
nest hiding there! Jacob was stung and I got a whip-
ping for the trouble we'd made. It seemed so unfair,
but eventually I realized that as the older of her sons I
was expected to be the responsible one.

Jay was home schooled as a boy because he suffered from what is now called attention deficit disor-
der. At six feet, four inches when he was just 16, Jay
was a great athlete, but he was also musical. He started
his own rock'n'roll band back when he was only 12 or
13, and the band became good enough to get paying
gigs.

Years later, as a college student in St. Johnsbury
in northern Vermont, Jay was skiing one winter's day
with some friends. On a race to the bottom, he collided
with one of his fellow skiers and broke his jaw.
Though he appeared to recover, the pain from his inju-
ries was so severe that he began taking prescriptive
opioids, to which he eventually became addicted. I was
a young adult by then, living on my own, when during

a California visit I received a call with the devasting news that he had died of an overdose. What made his death even more of a shock for me was the discovery that he had ignored the rehab arrangements I had made for him before my trip. Apparently he did not follow up because he was told his girl friend could not go with him. I will never know if my brother would still be alive had I not gone to California, something that I will live with for the rest of my life.

My father took Jay's death stoically, but it put your grandmother Persephone over the edge. She had long dealt with bouts of depression, but the loss of her only other child was more than she could bear and she lived the last years of her life with a constant sadness. Was she, she won- dered, somehow to blame for what had happened?

For me as well there would be questions I could not answer, but I was determined not to let them bring me down. I got over my grief in the same manner as I deal with all the problems in my life. The key is not to dwell on them, but to move forward. "What ifs" will destroy you. *You cannot change what is done, but you can make your future*: French Lesson Number Three!

After Jay died, I took solace from the experience of being loved, of remembering how important my mother and father had made me feel. Even the time when my mother had me assessed at Bellevue Hospital—she was, she said, worried that I was too cheerful—eventually struck me as a manifestation of her maternal concern for my wellbeing, however misguided in the instance of that evaluation. All the same, especially in the context of Jay's death, my mother's behavior taught me how vast are the chasms between extremes of human emotions, how mysterious the inner workings of the human heart.

I took nothing for granted and never have. Life was hard. But it was also beautiful, some-thing I hope to share later this week when I speak to my national Marcus & Millichap colleagues in a breakfast speech at the Union Club. I'll sign off now as I need to work on the draft of a talk I've given many times, making small changes on each occasion. My speech will be a version of one I've said many times, a variation on the children's story about the little engine that could. I was that little engine.

Now that I think about it, I suppose this may remind you three of advice I might have shared during family dinners when you were growing up. "There he goes again"—did you used to find yourself feeling like that when I started in on one of my favorite stories? I know I often felt like that as a boy in New Canaan. But what I remember now is not so much the specific words of something my parents said to me but the fact of that sharing, the fact that we were together and in the nurturing of those daily, meal-time gatherings I was learning something more important than the words themselves could teach me. I'm going to call this French Lesson Number Four: *By Your Presence Will You Be Known.* Through all their struggles, my mom and dad showed up. No matter what happened, I always knew they'd be there for me—as, I trust, you know I am and will be for you.

P.S. My dad was also the local scout master for 30 years, and he taught me and my friends how to enjoy the great outdoors. The skills he imparted enabled me later in life to become a mountain climber and to

take a group of people on an exploration of a rain for-
est…but let me not get too far ahead of myself here.

~

January 18

I am thinking now of the summer day after
my 17th birthday. I'd already learned to drive, and for
ten dollars at a junk yard I'd bought a "bugeye" Sprite
that could not be registered because it had and the
wheels were intact. In an open field on the New Canaan estate, around a single tree, I devised a race track
for my prized possession.

Sweet!

And I am thinking again of my father, who also
took care of two other estates, minding the flowers in
the greenhouse on one of them. A former student at an
agricultural college, he took multiple, first prizes at international flower shows in the city for his daffodils,
carnations, and orchids. How proud he was of those
awards! And how proud I was of him, a pride he be-
stowed on me—on all I did, on who I was…on who
we were.

Much later, in college, I would be born again

with a clean slate. "You can do anything you want to," I said to myself, "because you have no history." I would also learn that not being or doing what people expect is not a bad thing. You have to break stereotypes, but still be someone others can relate to. In college I moved into a dorm that was predominantly Jewish. I was a real outsider. When a group of us went out to dinner my classmates were amazed that I did not pick up the chicken we were served but, instead, cut if off the bone. They did not know I had been raised never to eat food with my fingers. That was one of many of the manners my parents stressed, and so I was never uncomfortable eating in someone else's home because I knew which fork to use! More profoundly, as I grew older I made it a point to learn other people's culture. The more you are exposed to different things the more you can relate to different people. Maybe I should call that French Lesson Number Five: *Know Thy Neighbor.*

Or maybe a different but related lesson is that you can never have too much class, though it's something I have never consciously worked on. What I did was build on that base of manners that my parents taught me: which is the right fork to use, hold a door open for a lady, write thank you notes. I later added to this foundation with an appreciation of wine, fine art, music, both because I enjoyed these things and because I discovered that other people were attracted to someone who possessed an educated culture—rather than, in my case, their perceiving me first and foremost as a person of color.

Back in New Canaan, years ago, I wondered who in fact were *we*…perhaps the poorest people of color in an affluent town populated mostly by well-off white folks. It wasn't something I thought about a great deal but, rather, was simply always aware of. Time and time again I would find myself in a situation where I realized I am the *only* "one" in the room—the only African-American. Like then, like now.

As a young child, I had my eyes open as I learned of the many different forms of racism. Some of it was mean spirited and some benign. It was hard for me to grasp that some people viewed blacks as lumped together in one group, living off welfare as their life choice. None of my family's relatives lived like that, even though they may not have had much money. When I was exposed to different racist situations, I tried to learn from them. I came to realize that there were people whose views I could not change, while others as I hoped might be more enlightened after meeting me. Over time, I felt that I had a great responsibility as a black person working his way through white America. At first I was angry, but eventually I decided that that emotion was not going to help me get ahead. You learn to ignore it and try to use it for your advantage.

There were of course other black families in New Canaan. Some of them, like mine, were what certain people might refer to as "the help," though neither my parents nor I ever used that term. There were also a few African-Americans who were professionals, and in New Canaan's single housing project a portion of the tenants were people of color, though I don't know the percentage—nor, I realize as I write this, was I sure what term to use to describe "us," as you can see from how I interchange. Why, in fact, do we even use such labels? I remember talking recently with a friend about sports announcers and he referred to so-and-so as that outspoken Afro-American personality, ditto several basketball stars, but when was the last time you heard someone say or write, "the white hockey hall-of-famer Wayne Gretzky?"

At school, there might have been three or four kids per class who were of color—to use the term I prefer, though in context like this it can sound awkward. Hints of racism were usually subtle, in what used to be termed an Amos 'n' Andy kind of way, which was a reference to a popular radio and television show that traded in racial stereotypes. But sometimes something more overt would occur. I remember coming home from school one day and telling my mother about a rhyme I had heard: "Eenie, menie, mynie, mo," it began, and I'm afraid we all know how the next line went.

Across from us on Smith Ridge Road was the New Canaan Country Club. A school friend whose family were members invited me to go swimming with him at the club. Something about a club rule regarding "the right color" made me think you were supposed to have a white bathing suit.

Wrong.

"And don't come back," I was told.

I learned the truth about what happened after my mother spoke with my friend's parents.

At that time I never thought I would someday become a member of a country club, let alone have golf as my great pastime. I was told in so many ways that such opportunities as owning my own home would never be mine—let alone a six-bedroom home in one of the wealthiest communities in the United States.

The only encouragement I received came from my parents, yet even with them there were limits on what they thought I could do, unwritten rules that I decided early on I was going to break. That said, I was very aware that I was an example of my race and therefore bore a great responsibility. Just the other day I was at a country music concert where I am sure I was the only person of color in attendance. You get used to the stare and people coming up to you thinking you must be someone famous. They are trying to figure out how a person who looks like me can be in the room.

I remember the second of the only two fistfights I have ever been in. A kid from Texas had moved into town and we ran into each other at the high school ballfield. This time I certainly knew the meaning of that word from that ugly rhyme. When he used it on me, I remembered a story my father had told me about two boys who had urinated on his bed in prep school. Like father, like son: I grabbed a baseball bat and threatened the Texas kid.

End of fight.

French Lesson Number Six: *You Do What You Have To Do*—even if it means disappointment for your best friend, someone in your family, or yourself, for that matter. And of course it's rarely a simple, isolated matter; everything happens in some kind of context, nothing stays the same. You need to be prepared and save up our strength and your resources, because a surprise, like a rainy day, will always come.

Take an example from my profession. I wake up on January first and I don't have a clue about what

I'm going to earn in the new year. Of course I can make an educated guess, but I live in fear of 2008 and 2009. I live in fear that what happened to our economy then will repeat. I have been fortunate to do what I do, but those years were horrific. At that time I owned my business, which I had to sell. I lost a couple of million dollars and came pretty close to being wiped out. I knew it was a matter of time and I did everything I could, but…all of you were still in school then, so a lot of my cash flow was going to tuitions. With my office here in White Plains, I also had people on my pay-roll—one of whom was of course one of you: Kate, who graduated from college in 2007 and began working for me in 2008, and then I had to lay you off.

I felt terrible, but that's part of being an entre-preneur. And it wasn't the first time I had gone through something like that. I will always remember the recession of 1986, which didn't fully impact me until I went into a pawn shop—first time in my life—with my gold Rolex in my hand. I'm feeling really down, about to pawn the watch to buy Christmas presents for our family…and then I started laughing, as I said to myself, "Why should I be feeling sorry for myself? I've got a gold Rolex that I can pawn. At least I can get through this recession."

By the way, I eventually got the watch back, and as you know—and as I will explain another time—I got back on a good track in business, though it took some doing, again doing what I had to do.

Even today, my team and I achieve success where others have failed. Just last year, we sold two Kmarts in secondary markets in deals that required us to do much more than send out an email blast and promote the properties on the Internet. In the first sale, the building was actually vacant, so we looked for a user rather than an investor, since this would result in a better profit for our seller. In the other case, Kmart was already operating with a short-term lease that included some options. With a question about the long-term viability of the business, we had to find a buyer who would still have a use for the property even if Kmart eventually leaves.

This has been a long letter, and I realize I've changed subjects midway—story of my life—but I just

FRENCH LESSONS

looked at my watch…got to go or I'll be late for my massage!

~

January 20

As much as I felt my racial identity, I was also keenly aware of my parents' financial situation. They were always in debt, often having to borrow money to cover even basic expenses. When my paternal grandfather died and left them an inheritance it was quickly spent, down to the last penny. And so I made a resolution: I will become financially independent. In a manner of speaking, I accomplished this while I was still a child.

It all started when someone gave me a hamster for a pet. I liked taking care of him so much that I saved up from my little allowance and bought another one, a female. When they mated, I put the litter's babies for sale. My hamster business was soon running a profit, and I opened an account at the New Canaan Savings Bank. To this day, I always save a portion of whatever I make. In the case of hamsters, I expanded my business by telling the people who bought hamsters from me that I would take care of them—for a fee—when they were away on vacation. I did this from about the age of six or seven until I was nine or 10 years old.

My next business was cinnamon tooth picks. I loved cinnamon. One day I discovered that if you soaked toothpicks in cinnamon oil they retained the flavor. So, I started selling the cinnamon tooth picks at school with my secret formula. My business exploded and I had a several sales people working for me for a per percentage of the sales. Pretty soon everyone in junior high was walking around with a toothpick in his or her mouth. Unfortunately, it did not take the school authorities very long to ban toothpicks in the school, because the used ones were left everywhere.

By then I had saved enough money, helping my father, to usher in my next business. Maybe more importantly I had also learned what I will share here as French Lesson Number Seven: *Create and you will be rewarded.* With my hamster and toothpick savings, lawn mowing, and some golf caddying, I soon bought my first motorcycle shortly after I got my driver's license. With the instate difference in tuition, by the time of my graduation I was able to finance the purchase of water beds that I sold for a nice profit. Eventually, after the Adams family forgave my student loans, I bought my parents a house.

I'm making a note to myself to share more on those water beds in another letter. Got to run.

~

January 27

As a student, I didn't necessarily thrive in high school. High school was hard for me, because as a person of color I did not feel that I belonged to any group, so I created an outsider group which kids thought was cool. I drove too fast and took chances. With some friends I snuck onto the town reservoir, where someone dared me to jump off a 60-foot cliff. I did it, even though I was not a good swimmer. I did not realize how hard water could feel until I hit it, but luckily I did not break anything. Those where the darkest years of my life, being told that my opportunities were limited and feeling that I did not belong. Our country was in a great racial turmoil, and as a teenager I did not know how to deal with it.

I was the Fonzie of my class, and I know that name dates me. Fonzie, or the Fonz, was a happy-go-lucky character in a sitcom called *Happy Days*. I continued to push limits. Rode to school on my motorcycle. The drinking age was only 18 at that time in nearby New York state, so I created a false ID—it stated I was from South Africa—in order to buy beer. I did some serious partying. Senior year I didn't work too hard, visited the library only occasionally, and failed trigonometry. I was told by my guidance counselor that I "wasn't college material." But I never thought I wasn't going to college. I went to summer school and was accepted by the one college to which I applied, Belknap in Center Harbor, N.H.

Would you believe I made the dean's list my first (and only) year at Belknap? I spent more time on the ski slopes at nearby Gunstock, where I had a season pass, than I did attending classes. My weekly schedule during the winter was three days of school, four days on the ski slopes. Later I used that skill, combined with a growing fascination with photography, to parlay a gig as the official, on-slope photographer at Smuggler's Notch in northern Vermont.

My mom had exposed me to skiing. With hand-me-downs from a family friend, I drove with her from New Canaan to the Berkshires, where we'd stay in a lodge or an inexpensive motel. Skiing soon became my favorite sport. I loved going downhill as fast as I could, carving through the snow, especially if it was fresh powder. My mother was also the person who got me started in tennis, a sport I played into middle age, before I discovered golf. As I tell my associates, I am not a great golfer but I have made millions of dollars playing golf! But all the sports I played have in some related way helped me in business, even if only as conversation starters. Meet a stranger on the plane, it's unlikely he or she wants to hear how a shopping center is financed. But tell them you are a serious cyclist and chances are you'll soon be sharing something more important—a lead to a new client, an idea for a brochure. My mother must have known this, because she was a big believer that sports were a way for me to get ahead in life, not to mention staying healthy.

Back in New Canaan as a boy, I played Little League baseball, though my season was shortened the summer I was ten years old. Persephone had two siblings who lived in Oklahoma. She wanted to visit them and she wanted me to meet them, so off we went in our 1955 Chevy with my little brother and my cousin named Ron. I brought along some hamsters, too!

Crossing through Arkansas, we stopped for the night at a motel that AAA recommended, but we were turned away because the motel was "no colored." We ended up sleeping in the car, and the next morning, as we crossed into Oklahoma, we looked for a place to do some laundry, only to be told by some native Americans that "no colored were allowed." It shocked me that other people of color—native Americans—would be prejudiced against people like myself.

Nevertheless, the trip proved beneficial to my baseball l career, because my Oklahoma uncle was a great coach and worked with me on my hitting. I was just a second-string player, but playing every day in a field behind my uncle's church made me a star! When we returned in August to New Canaan, I went three for three in the local Little League "world series" and was named my team's most valuable player. Practice, I learned, really does make a difference. If you want to succeed at something, you have to work at it, and then you may achieve even more than you have imagined in your dreams.

This was a lesson I remembered years later when the New Hampshire ski season came to a close. I had made great progress academically, and the following fall I transferred to the University of Connecticut. By the time I had applied for student housing, none was available. Frustrated, I became a day student at the university's Stamford campus, where I struggled. I found living at home to be too much of a distraction. Remembering how well my grandfather had done at the University of Southern Illinois in Carbondale, my mom suggested I transfer there. I was reluctant to move again, but sometimes change is the only choice. As it turned out, this choice, to follow my mother's advice, was the right one. French Lesson Number Eight: *When something's not working, fix it.*

FRENCH LESSONS

Chapter 2

Know Thyself and
Find Your Path

Dear Beautiful Daughters,

French Lesson Number Ten may be an old one in anyone's book, but that doesn't lessen the importance: *Know who you are.*

It's Saturday afternoon as I write this. Stopped at the club this morning to hit some balls in our pro's indoor simulator. Of course it's not the same as real golf, but it helps to keep me limber during the off season and I enjoy the routine. Plus ever since your mom got me to try Bikram Yoga I've noticed a big change in my ability to make a good turn as I take the club back. Sorry to get technical there, but you're all such good athletes I know you'll understand.

Sometimes when I meet a person who doesn't play, I have to explain to them what a boon to my business golf has been...I'm an amateur, I tell them, but I've made more money on the course than many professionals! And that's not even counting what golf gives me back in terms of a better focus and good feeling in everything else I do. Even a bad day at the course, when my game isn't as sharp as I wish, makes me feel happy.

And I love coming back here to the office afterwards, which is where I am now. It's empty, which is part of the appeal. Much as I like being with other people, there is a sense of refuge on these quiet Saturdays, when I can catch up on something I may not have finished during the week and begin to strategize about what lies ahead. I take my time, like the lyric of that famous blues song. French Lesson Number Nine: *Never rush unless you have to.*

Being here like this also helps me reflect on the proverbial balance between good days and not-so-good (I dislike using the word bad). We're all often in such a hurry that such reflection also enables me to see something about myself…my "story," as the saying goes…which more than anything else I wish to share with you. To get where I am, life has been my teacher and still is. Along the way, there have been many aha moments, going back even to my early adulthood, when I was trying to figure out my skills and how best to use them.

My story, then, is nothing less than life, both its

ups and downs, and how I have adapted to change. More than once I have realized how differently things could have gone, how easily in a certain situation I could have failed. In one of the worst financial calamities this country faced—the recession in the late 1980s—I wasn't alone, but many others came out pretty screwed up. I lost a lot, but I was also by then the father of two of you—Kate and Eliza, with Chloe still to come—so even though I have always been a risk taker, I decided to risk my time but not my money…but once again, I'm getting ahead of myself.

To go back a bit: you may remember my mentioning last month that soon after graduating from college I combined my love of skiing and my growing skill as a photographer and went to work for the Smugglers Notch resort in northern Vermont. At that point in my young adulthood, I was feeling pretty free. In college I'd been exposed to new realms of people and place. With my major in psychology, I'd even daydreamed about continuing my formal education with a Ph. D. But my mom's mental health was not stable— she'd been in and out of several institutions—and so I was already feeling the responsibility and need to make some money. I knew I needed to support myself, and down the road I might need to help the parents who had sacrificed for my wellbeing.

When I think about this period in my life, especially when someone asks me a question about my "secret"—as if there were some uncanny explanation for what has enabled me to make and then act upon certain kinds of decisions that others did not—I am often left with the image of certain athletes I admire. Take, for example, the golfer Fred Couples, whose smooth, supple swing has long been the envy of anyone who plays the game. A friend told me about an interview during which Fred was asked how he shaped his shots—how, that is to say, he was able to hit the ball on demand so it went straight or curving left (a draw) or right (a fade). Instead of the mechanical answer involving grip or ball position you might expect, Couples instead explained that he simply decided where he wanted the ball to end up and then made the swing that would enable that intention. Pure instinct, in other words, but of course based upon a rigorous, schooled technique.

Not to compare myself to Fred—especially on the golf course, lol—but something about his explanation strikes me as profound. We all need what musicians call chops, without which no one would want to listen to whatever a particular singer or instrumentalist was performing. But chops alone do not make a musician, anymore than technique itself does not enable an athlete to excel.

I remember a conversation with a friend who became an administrator in higher education, someone whose duties included serving as spokesperson for one of the most prestigious such institutions in the United States. What had this man first done upon his own graduation from college? Laid bricks for a friend who was a mason; done barn chores for a farmer; filled in as a substitute teacher for schools near where he lived. When I heard about those gigs, I immediately thought of my time at Smugglers Notch…and, though the two may not seem to go together, my admiration for Fred Couples.

Before I explain, let me make clear I have great respect for masonry, farming, and teaching! How could I not? And hard as I work on it, I wish my golfing skills were sharper. What I'm driving at here is something else, a certain *je ne sais quoi*, if you will, that makes possible the ability to be, to do, within the framework of whatever is at hand—in life—whether you're finding your way as a young adult, recently graduated from college, or a famous athlete getting older but continuing to play at a high level. And so, even when I was smoking a little weed as I waited for the next skier to stop and have his or her picture taken, a sense of who I was that had been impressed upon me since childhood was operative subliminally, just as it had when I was selling waterbeds the summer after I graduated from college.

That reminds me I mentioned waterbeds earlier. Let me explain.

One of my college classmates showed me an ad for a closeout sale of waterbeds. So, I sold my car and motorcycle and used the proceeds to buy a tractor trailer load of 400 waterbeds. When the truck came to the estate were I was again staying with my parents, it could not negotiate the curve in the driveway. We had to unload the truck and then re-load each waterbed in my parents' station wagon before ferrying each one of them to the three-car garage over which my family lived. We then stacked them from floor to ceiling.

Whatever prompted me to think this wasn't a fool's errand? But guess what: I paid seven dollars a piece for those waterbeds and sold them for…forty! If you do the math—and remember, this was in 1970 dollars—I grossed just over $13,000. Subtract the cost of $2,800, financed as I mentioned by the sale of car and motorcycle, and a hundred or so I paid the friend who helped me unload them, and I made a profit of about $10,000…half of which I used as a down payment on a $50,000, two-family home in Ridgefield, Connecticut that I sold a year later for $100,000!

French Lesson Number Eleven: *Look first, but remember to leap.*

~

February 10

So sorry…I was getting to something about waterbeds when I realized I was going to be late for dinner and…now a week has passed! I'm in my deserted office again—it's another Saturday—and not to look at myself in a metaphorical mirror, but I just got my hair cut by the only person I know who does it right and…she did an especially good job today - :)

Vanity, vanity, but I mention this for two, re-lated reasons: poor as we were when I was growing up in New Canaan, my mother always made certain that both Jacob and I were bathed and well dressed. To this day, my morning's ritual has changed very little, re-minding me always of Persephone. And whatever one's walk in life, I believe the presentation you make in your appearance has a bearing on your success—not because of the money you may have spent on your clothes, but as a manifestation of the focus you have given to whatever you are about to do. Of course clothes don't truly make the man or woman, but like haircut, like ambition…or, as the former pro at the club of a friend told my friend: "just because you can't play a lick, at least look like you can." French Lesson Number Twelve: *First impressions are important.*

Funny thing about those waterbeds: going back to my hamsters, they were certainly not the first idea

I'd had that made me some money, but up until then they were far and away the most profitable. Soon afterwards, however, they were eclipsed…by Cadillacs and Jaguars

Turns out that the grandfather of one of my high school classmates, Kim Bradley, was the chairman of General Motors, and his father owned a General Motors dealership in the nearby town of Norwalk that needed a salesman. Kim talked his dad in to hiring me, even though I was of course young and all the other salesmen were middle-aged or older. Nor, at that time in Fairfield County, did people of color sell cars at high-end dealerships.

As all three of you know, I've always been something of a car guy, not just as a driver but as someone familiar with how they work. As I was soon to learn, in addition to self-knowledge, knowing the details of a product is such a huge advantage that I share it with you as French Lesson Number Thirteen: *Knowledge is key*.

On my very first day as a car salesman, a guy came into the showroom wanting to buy a Chrysler.

"Sir," I said. "We don't sell that here, but may I show you an Oldsmobile?"

"It's not what I'm looking for. What's so special about an Oldsmobile?"

As soon as he said that I knew that I had him, because I was able to share with him detail by detail the difference between a Chrysler V-8 and an Olds, how each car handled, what made the Olds transmission superior…even why the headlights were better designed!

Would you be surprised if I reported that he bought an Olds?

But he wasn't the only person who did! On one historic day—historic in my six-month auto salesman career—I sold twelve cars. All told, I saved enough money to buy myself a BMW and take off for that gig at Smugglers Notch without a worry about how I would support myself on days I didn't sell any skier photographs. And when the ski season ended in April, I still had enough money in my savings account to follow a woman I'd met…hey, I was single…to follow her to Ecuador, where she was going to study during the summer at the university in the country's capital, Quito.

How I loved living in a country in which I never experienced racism. I learned Spanish, and when my friend left for the States I moved in with a family who basically adopted me. I had my own quarters in their guest house, and we became so close that to this day I feel that had I stayed longer than a year I could still be there, taking breaks to climb the nearby, scenic mountains, and perhaps running an import business (U.S.-manufactured camping equipment was especially popular back then). Eventually, however, I started feeling a little homesick. And, as my photography skills continued to improve, I wondered if I might actually embark on a career as an artist. As I was soon to learn, the shortest distance between two points—not on a map, but in your life—is not a straight line.

French Lesson Number Fourteen: *Learn from the detours*.

~

February 24

Yikes! Out of town for a several days—first on

a business trip to Puerto Vallarta (where I also got to play some golf) and then on the way home with a stop in Florida (where I met up with your mom), we returned to a house without heat—the furnace had died while we were gone. Luckily, with the crazy weather we've been having, none of the pipes froze. But this does present a challenge, with our plans to sell the house, probably moving out of Bronxville, and downsizing to something that makes more sense for us, now that you've all flown the coop. Do we try to get the furnace repaired or invest in a new one? Such questions…the stuff of domestic life. But they come up in business, too.

The photography I did during my "time out" in Vermont was made possible in large part by the gift of a camera that my parents made upon my college graduation. But the idea of becoming a photographer had been planted much earlier. As long ago as I can remember, I had been an observer. I was forever watching other people, and I had developed a keen eye for how they behaved, what they wore, how they interacted with one another, what one person looked like in repose, another in action. And, in the context of my New Canaan childhood, I was fascinated by the physical difference between, say, the garden my father kept on the Adams estate where we lived and the rush of traffic in the center of town, or a comparison between the foliage at the estate's entrance and a lone tree in the front yard of my high school.

With the gift of my camera, I was able to begin documenting what I saw. Always fascinated as well with how things work, I quickly became adept at playing with the aperture openings and light settings. I was basically unschooled in the deeper aspects of what had remained mostly a pastime, but after returning from Ecuador I began to dream might become something more. I started hanging out at a local photographer's school, where I eventually took some classes. That enabled me to meet several famous photographers who were the school's teachers. Never one to refrain from a reasonable risk, I decided to go all in and enrolled in a photography course in Yosemite, taught by the great Ansel Adams.

I think it was the legendary catcher for the New

York Yankees, Yogi Berra, who is reputed to have said: "When you reach a fork in the road, take it." Or as your dad—c'est moi—would phrase it, as French Lesson Number Fifteen: *Stop, look, and if it looks good, chance it.*

As an Adams student, I was assigned to go out into the woods with my 4x5 camera and be observant. You have to remember, this was in the 1970s, an era when it seemed clothes were often optional. There were a number of nude women in the woods whom we pretended to ignore until an instructor named Judy Dater—who would become an established photographer in her own right—explained that our assignment was to photography them. It turned out that such an exotic but ultimately arduous discipline taught me the difference between what the late critic Kenneth Clark called naked versus nude. The former, he said, meant the exposure that comes with no clothes, while the latter, as a work of art, had no such explicit connotation.

Such theory notwithstanding—and I would be fibbing if I said there was not anything erotic about such an experience—the real exposure for me was the dawning realization that I could utilize my eye and the contacts I made through Adams to acquire photographs by others...and sell them. At that time, the market for most photography was still in its infancy, with few photographers able to sell their work for much more than $100 an image. Though at the time I was studying my biggest purchase was a thousand dollars for an Edward Weston print that I quickly sold for twice that amount, I hit a home run with an inexpensive Adams print that I sold for $65,000.

My insight here was the hunch that vintage photography would eventually become a good market. I remember sitting in a little cabin in Yosemite as Ansel played the piano, and even then I had a sixth sense that there was something special about this man and his art. Nevertheless, after my first good sale, I was afraid I might have overspent on the FedEx shipping charge!

Gradually, as I put my own camera away, I acquired prints by such other artists as Imogen Cunningham and Eliot Porter. But my biggest coup was the purchase of several prints by Berenice Abbott, following which I travelled to Maine, where I called on her at her studio. We became friends, and eventually she made me her dealer, which led me finally to open a gallery in Manhattan.

By then—how all this seemed suddenly to come together in a way I could never have imagined—I dabbled in the music business, and all along continued to acquire real estate. I lived frugally, and by my 30th birthday could already call myself a millionaire. But I was restless and, if truth be told, a little unmoored.

Chapter 3

Turbulent Times

March 4

My Dears,

Just back from church…it's a Sunday for a change, and I'm headed shortly for lunch at the club and then a quick stop at the office…but I know I left you hanging at the end of my last. I hereby pledge to make the time for a longer letter, but before I forget I want to remind you of some advice I just gave a friend, which I suppose we might called French Lesson Number Sixteen: *never talk in an elevator*! I learned that the hard way.

Got to run, but much more to come, very soon! I love you.

~

March 10

Ok, as promised…as I was starting to say about elevators: you never know who may be eavesdropping on the details of a deal you're in the midst of, nor is this really just a matter of being in a place such as an elevator that is public. The larger point, to restate an old adage, is to keep your own counsel, by which I

mean wherever you are and however you are communicating, think twice before speaking.

I remember well the impact of reading the
works of the great Ralph Ellison, not just his master-
piece, *Invisible Man*, but an essay a friend shared with
me called "Little Man at Chehaw Station." It made
such an impression on me.

As a young man, Ellison was studying at the
Tuskegee, where he was actually a music major. One
day, after apparently disappointing some of the faculty
members with his performance at a recital, the future
author went to see Hazel Harrison, a teacher who was
also a fine pianist.

Ellison reports that she reminded him of a tru-
ism—that you always have to play your best—to
which Ellison said of course! Then Ms. Harrison said
there was more to it than that.

> "*...you must* always *play your best,
> even if it's in the waiting room at
> Chehaw Station, because in this country
> there'll always be a little man behind the
> stove.*"

"A what?"

"She nodded.

"That's right,"' she said. "There'll always be the little man whom you don't expect, and he'll know the music, and the tradition, and the standards of musician-ship required for whatever you set out to perform!"

As you know, I love music, thought I'm no musician. But, of course, music's not really the point of the story. Chehaw Station could be anywhere. And the Ellison's little man could be anyone.

~

March 11

Good morning! Your mother called just as I was writing to remind me we were going out and so I pressed save but didn't send and now we're off to church, but I'll try to pick up where I left off this afternoon.

~

March 17

So much for my good intentions…I ended up

taking a long call and…you know the drill! Story of my working life. So, here I am again, back at the office of a Saturday afternoon. It's now St. Patrick's day, though if truth be told I'm not sure if I know who that Patrick was and why he's called a saint. And I must further confess that I'm not wearing green. Ah, but of course…Saint Patrick goes with Ireland, one of my favorite destinations (for golf, lol).

As all three of you know, I love music, but I'm neither musician nor artist, unless we were to define the art more broadly, something I'd like to circle back at another time, in a different letter. But I quoted Ellison last week because his parable of the "little man" strikes me as the flip side of my advice about not talking in an elevator: yes, we all want to be careful of what we say to whom, but at the same time we also must strive to be our very best in every situation. As a jazz musician put it in a book published several years ago, "I play the same, whether it's Carnegie Hall in New York City or Carnegie Hall in Lewisburg, West Virginia."

French Lesson Number Seventeen: *Treat every-one the same.*

By the time I read that book I knew enough of the real estate business to understand the reference to West Virginia first hand. As I wrote you a few weeks ago, by the early 1980s I was beginning to feel it was time to bring some order and clarity to a life and career that so far had brought me much enjoyment and financial success but scant feeling of greater purpose. In a word, as a professional I was peripatetic.

The election of Ronald Regan was the beginning of what I now would call my turbulent years, even though as they transpired I knew I had finally found the foundation of what would guide my work ever after. With the ascendency of Reagan, the collectibles market that I'd become a part of was to be heavily hit in the early 1980's. This was because of a change in our country's tax laws—the Economic Recovery Tax Act of 1981—that was accompanied by a recession and high interest rates. The art had boom of the 1970's had occurred largely because of inflation and a rapid increase in art values. With the changes that followed, part of my wealth in art was eroded by a decline in value. I started to think about other ways to make money.

Voila! Was it fate or coincidence? I will never know, but one day in 1983 a childhood friend, Scott Brown, stopped by my gallery. The last time I had seen him he was driving an old VW beetle and selling vacuum cleaners. Now he was in my gallery looking to buy art for his home in Connecticut and his apartment in the city. After he bought several pieces, I helped him load everything into his new BMW.

"What kind of work have you been doing?" I asked him.

"Office leasing," he replied. "I just closed a deal with a million dollar commission."

This, as the saying goes, was when a million dollars was a million dollars.

Wanting to limit my present financial exposure. I asked Scott if he were hiring. He warned me that the real estate business was racist, but when he realized I was serious, he gave me a cubicle. Nevertheless, he kept telling me there was only one other person in the entire city in this business who looked like me. Before I left several years later there were two more, who were actually brothers.

The first deal that I actually did started when I got on the phone. There were of course no personal computers, but we did have floppy-disk IBM computers and calculators. Excel hadn't been invented yet, but we had a primitive program that you could do numbers with, a hugely important tool because the market in New York was very complicated. Here's an example: porters had a very strong union, and they would sign long contracts…five years, as I recall. These contracts had nothing specific to do with a tenant, but they certainly added a cost factor to prospective leases because a typical lease included the stipulation that the rent would increase annually by whatever factor the wage for porters had increased.

Another complication was the difference between the total square footage of a leased space (which is called rentable square feet) and the portion of that overall space that is actually useable square feet. So, in such a scenario, that total square footage might include an oddly shaped area or the entrance/egress for an elevator, neither of which could be used in the actual place for whatever business the lessee conducted.

That said, a landlord might make every effort to charge a tenant for the entire space, putting the person handling the negotiation—yours truly—in an unenviable position. So, in my new gig, the first person to whom I show a space hires an architect to design how the person's business will be configured in the space—the buildout, this is called—which has to be approved by the landlord. Meanwhile, the architect explains the useable portion of the space, and my client flips out, accusing me of cheating! I tried to explain, but his was a small business and he was unsophisticated about how the system worked.

I lost that deal.

But I soon succeeded with many others, beginning with some deals for federal government office space on Staten Island. In both instances—one involving the IRS, the other Social Security—the tenant was looking for a turnkey space, which is one wherein the space is basically ready to go from the start. And with the prospect at the time of inflation, I was able to negotiate rent that was high enough to cover future inflation.

My feet were now wet, so to speak, and soon I had an opportunity to work on much larger deals that in some cases Scott had initiated. One was for a space located near Grand Central Station and partially occupied by the editorial offices of *Architectural Digest*. Though the magazine had rented most of the building, it only used about half of the space, which was set aside for future

expansion. This gave me an opportunity to work with a tenant who was acting as a landlord, since I was subleasing the extra space and then getting a deal approved by the landlord.

As Scott developed relationships with people such as Mesulam Riklis, an Israeli businessman who did leveraged buyouts, I handled the job of subleasing vacant space after Scott moved a company into smaller, cheaper space. For example, he took control

of Faberge, located in at 1345 Avenue of the Americas. Faberge had office space totaling 70,000 square feet on two floors. The chairman's office alone was 5,000 square feet, more than enough room for a grand piano, complete drum set, and seats and music stands for a small orchestra! The president's office had its own bathroom with gold fixtures, and the president's desk was on a pedestal, so when a visitor sat in a chair he or she was lower than the
president, as if to make sure the person realized their supposedly less important standing in life.

Scott ended up relocating part of the Faberge company to Mahwah, New Jersey. Working with Scott and his colleague, David Itzkowitz—who taught me everything I knew about office leasing—we also moved Mr. Riklis into 25,000 square feet in Trump tower. I remember both Riklis and Trump bragging about how much money their casinos made.

All in all, this was a hard business to succeed in. Much of the time, you had to call on people who didn't really want to talk with you. There was also the constant challenge of finding a new use for an old space versus finding new spaces. I would sometimes take an elevator to the top floor of a building, write down the name of each tenant as I walked down, floor by floor, and then knock on doors, hoping to meet a business's decision maker.

Meanwhile, as the art market crashed after the enactment of those Reagan tax changes, something wonderful happened: your mother and I became engaged. I will write about how we met in another letter, but the moment was bittersweet because at almost the same time my father developed cancer. He died in May of 1984 and your mother and I were married two months later, in July. That fall, she became pregnant with the oldest of you three, Katharine.

Again, the moment was bittersweet, as Mrs. Adams, having lost both her husband and my father, put the New Canaan estate on the market. Alas, I had to negotiate with her for some sort of termination payment for my mother. She offered $10,000, and I reminded her that my father had run the estate for 30 years and his widow deserved better. Mrs. Adam had a problem in that the estate was under contract and she need my mother out of her space. Without my help that was never going to happen in a timely manner. This gave me the ability to negotiate a reasonable settlement.

Now I had the stress of getting her out. My mother was a hoarder and was sure she was going to win the *Reader Digest* Sweepstakes! This required the purchase of many magazines, one of which—truth be told—was my subscription to *Playboy*. She never threw out any of these magazines. In previous years my father and I would take a station wagon load to the recycling plant once a year. To fulfill my promise to Mrs. Adams to relocate my mother took teamwork. I had a dumpster positioned outside my mother's bedroom window. Maureen took my mother on a drive and while they were gone I threw things out the window. I also knew I had to find a place that she was willing to live in, and after much searching I finally located an apartment in Sheldon, Connecticut.

By then, I had hired someone to run my art business as a private dealer. And I was looking for a place to raise our family, finally settling on a brown-stone on 94th Street between Columbus and Central Park West.

I also purchased more rental properties in Connecticut, since borrowing money then was very easy. In 1985, I decided to make my brownstone into a co-op, a two-year process that required approval from the office of the Attorney General of the State of New York.

~

March 18

The Tax Reform Act of 1986 changed my world forever. It was the beginning of a recession that affected the real estate business for many years. Every crash as it impacts real estate is finally and foremost about the availability of money. In 1986 I sold our weekend house in Connecticut to buy our house in Bronxville. I had assumes the sale of a brownstone as a co-op would be easy, but I had not understood the full impact of another change in the Tax Reform Act. Eventually, I had to put a large mortgage on the property to renovate all the apartments and take my profits out before I sold the units. But no one, it turned out

was eager to buy. And the office leasing

market had become soft.

When I realized that I was unlikely to sell any

units, you may recall my starting to share in an earlier

letter that I went to Marine Midland (now HSBC) and

asked for a reduction of my 15 percent rate to the pre-

sent market rate of ten percent. The bank officer's re-

sponse was not helpful.

"You have never been late, let alone missed a

payment," he said. "So, we are not going to help you,

because you are not a problem loan."

They never received another payment from me.

The bank then tried to sell my loan to a money

launderer for the Genovese crime family. He finessed a

deal of fifty cents on the dollar. My lawyer and I then

met with him and his lawyer. We knew who he was

and made it clear it was not going to be easy for him to

get face value for the loan out of me. He did not pro-

ceed with buying my loan. The market was so soft that

it was

unclear if he would have to have foreclosed to get his

money out, and the hassle of going after me for the balance appeared not to be not worth the trouble.

I was then able to buy the loan for the same price from the bank. At that point, I stopped paying all the rest of my loans and did work outs. There was so much turmoil in the banking world then that none of my defaults were reported to the credit agency. I would meet with a bank and the next week they would be out of business and I would then wait months, sometimes a year, before someone would contact me about one of my loans.

On top of all this, my mother suffered a diabetic stroke, and I had to find a nursing home for her. When I called and asked several places if they had availability, they all said yes. But when I then visited, I was told they were suddenly full. I soon realized that because I was black the nursing homes assumed I had no money and my mother would therefore be on Medicaid, which paid less than what the nursing home could charge privately. Only when I made certain to tell management that we could afford to pay the rack rate did a room become available.

P.S. I've been scribbling notes now and then, musings that form a collection of somewhat random thoughts I want to share; they connect in various ways to what I learned during the era of my office leasing, which I've come to think of as the turbulent part of life, not just in work but how work crossed with so many aspects of the period when I also gave up going solo.

They constitute not so much a litany of more lessons as, instead, a kind of road map that helped chart my course through all that turbulence and to which I turn today, often reflexively, much as one grooves a golf swing over many years of practice and playing:

- changing gears when you come home, putting that day's work in a mental pocket;

- communicating, not assuming whatever you've just done or are about to do is clear to colleagues;

- making a list—like these bullet points—before a call and the keeping them uppermost in mind with trigger words that prompt memory;

FRENCH LESSONS

- strategizing before you meet a client, even about how you should dress;

- knowing the product…knowing the product…knowing the product;

- knowing the customer;

- being informed about other things, well enough to converse about them but never in a way that sounds superior;

- remembering that the people you are working with on a deal are probably not the only people with a stake in the deal;

- living cheaply, in our own case in that brownstone with income coming from other real estate, so a bad month or even a bad year could be weathered;

- embracing the roller-coaster financial life of constant change;

- never forgetting the old adage that time is money;

- gauging each deal with solid information to form the right pitch;

- paying constant attention to the details;

FRENCH LESSONS

- reading tone of voice and body language;
- adjusting to different personalities; and,
- using the experience of each new deal to sharpen one's skill set.

It just occurred to me that the thread running through these thought *is* another lesson, number 18: *Be Prepared*.

~

March 24

The end of my office leasing career could be a Seinfeld episode, though I didn't see the humor at the time:

I get an exclusive to relocate a 15,000 square-foot tenant. The commission is going to be $250,000, more at that point in my career than I have ever made on anything else for a single deal.

If they renew I do not get paid.

They tell me they are never renewing.

"They" are a branch office for an Ohio base printing company.

I show the regional manager a number of spaces.

After a couple of months, we identify a space in the Graybar Building.

It is a great building, attached to Grand Central.

We negotiate the terms of the lease, including everything but an upgraded carpet for the regional manager's office.

Big mistake.

The executive vice president calls to say he is coming to town with the executed lease and we are to meet for lunch.

I get a call later in the morning that he needs to change our meeting until cocktail hour.

I meet him for drinks.

The executive vice president tells me that I am the best broker he has ever worked with.

I negotiated a great deal for his company, he says.

The existing landlord will match the deal and upgrade the carpet, he adds.

He offers me $300 for my time.

"You can keep your money," I tell him.

I buy the drinks.

French Lesson Number Nineteen: *Listen to the person with the primary interest.*

French Lesson Number Twenty: *Take care of the person with the primary interest.*

After that experience, I decided that office leasing was not for me. It's a tough game, and I was thinking now that I would have to make a lot of money very quickly to continue. More profoundly, you—my daughters, me, anyone really—want in whatever you do to feel good each morning about where you're going, what you're about to do. So, in my own case, I knew I couldn't do this for the rest of my life.

But I'm not going to leave real estate, I decide. No, I'm going to branch out, extend my reach, find a way to use my knowledge and skills and make calls to people who will want to speak with me. You could call this my most important, business aha moment: there's got to be more to real estate, I realized, than leasing office space. In personal life, I had invested in real estate not because I knew anything special, but had more or less stumbled on it. Perhaps, I thought, if I got some more education I might discover there was something else I could do.

But first I'm going to have to earn a new degree—a degree in real estate. I applied to a program at NYU and was accepted. Forty years old, and now the proud father of two daughters, I was going back to school.

But I didn't immediately quit the gig with Scott…and even when I finally did I didn't cut the cord completely. To this day, I get together once a year for lunch with his other associates, all of whom also eventually left the company. In fact, we call the event our Scott Brown lunch.

Chapter 4

Best Friends

April 7

Spring at last! Or should I say, "spring still," after the weather we enjoyed in London? And what a joy it was to be together! Chloe, maybe you should see if your graduate program can be extended another year, so we will have an official excuse to keep visiting…not, of course, that we really need such.

Now that I'm back, and before I share with you the big break in my career and the transition it enabled into the business I'm still a part of, I want to press the pause button for a moment.

With your implicit blessing, I want to return to a moment and person in my life when everything changed. In my experience, a career doesn't happen in isolation from one's personal life.

They are intertwined, like the weavings of past and present.

Everything connects.

To be continued…I'm still catching up.

~

April 14

Where was I?

FRENCH LESSONS

Most of all, right here, I'd like to give myself permission to say something most people might think out of character—in a good way, please—for someone in my business…as if there were a "type" for characters like your father. There are no types. We are each unique, even within our family, you three, your mother, and I.

Whether looking out my office window, taking the long way from White Plains to Bronxville, or traveling as I still do (though not like I once did, at times in my life away more than home)…or even sitting quietly, immobile, as I imagine or remember…the image of buildings with which I have had an association—as leasing agent or investment advisor—inspires within me an abiding sense of the lives that both created and now use them.

As a former student of Ansel Adams, I need no reminder of our country's natural beauty. I love the out of doors, a windswept mountaintop vista, a desert landscape of sand and stone, sagebrush and cactus. But when I see or recall the lights in an office building's windows or the cars in a shopping center's parking lot,

I think first and foremost of the people they represent…the people with whom I may have dealt, doing a deal, and those whom I may never know who now occupy or use what I helped make.

Beauty indeed!

There are those in our country who would decry what I've just written, as if we might return to an era of the general store, with a wood stove keeping customers warm in the winter, penny candy for sale behind the counter, rocking chairs arranged in pairs on the porch. I suppose in such a scenario we might rip up our concrete highways and toss away our cellphones. Hitch up that horse to the buggy. Bring back silent movies.

But not to debate, nor do I wish to preach about progress. What I'm trying to convey is the human wonder that even a lowly discount mart represents. Think if you will of the infrastructure that makes it possible and then reflect on the fact that it, too, is part of a phenomenon that we can so easily take for granted: the relative ease of reaching it, the bounty on its shelves, the ubiquity of its identity. All made possible because of people.

Have any of you read or seen a production of a once-popular play, *Our Town*, by an author named Thornton Wilder? Whatever blind ideal Mr. Wilder may have had in mind as the model for the place he called Grover's Corners, there is no denying the power of the moment in the third act when one of the main characters, a woman named Emily, returns to earth after her untimely death.

"Let's really look at one another!...It goes so fast," she says. "We don't have time to look at one another. I didn't realize. So all that was going on and we never noticed...Wait! One more look. Good-bye , Good-bye world. Good-bye, Grover's Corners....Mama and Papa. Good-bye to clocks ticking....and Mama's sunflowers. And food and coffee. And new ironed dresses and hot baths....and sleeping and waking up. Oh, earth, you are too wonderful for anybody to realize you. Does anyone ever realize life while they live it...every, every minute?"

I love the stylistic repetition of that common

word, "every." How I wish I could respond with my own double affirmative: "yes, yes." But I try. What more can any of us do?

Perhaps that might be a way for me to explain how I met my best friend—your mother—half my lifetime ago.

Back in 1981, Mary John—the sister of someone I knew—invited me dinner to help celebrate the birthday of her friend Maureen Casey. Also at the party was Maureen's then boyfriend. I vividly remember how beautiful and smart she was! Afterwards, I could not stop talking about her, but knowing about that boyfriend I kept my distance. Then, as if fate intervened, I was invited to go skiing with both Mary John and Maureen. Now I was really smitten. Soon afterwards, at another party with Mary John, I learned that Maureen had broken up with her boyfriend. I could hardly contain my excitement over this news.

"Would you like to have dinner?" Maureen asked.

"Are there stars out tonight?" I thought but, containing myself, simply replied, "yes!"

FRENCH LESSONS

On that first date, Maureen pointed out something that to this day has impacted my life. We were heading along Storrow Drive in Boston when I misread a traffic sign.

"Are you dyslexic?" Maureen asked.

Up to then, I had never heard the word. All those years ago I had struggled in school, but no one had observed that I exhibited the traits of someone with dyslexia. Learning this and discovering that other people also suffered from dyslexia was a both tremendous relief and a boost to my self-esteem. Not to compare, but I was in the company of such greats as Albert Einstein and Pablo Picasso!

I moved to Boston for the summer, and we spent a lot of time together. In the fall, I moved back to Connecticut but rented a house in Vermont, where we started meeting on weekends. The following summer, as a special education teacher, Maureen was on vacation for two months. Off we went to Paris! At the end of summer I asked her to marry me…and she said yes!

That fall, my father was rushed to the hospital with a perforated ulcer. While he was in the hospital the doctors discovered that he also had kidney cancer which had spread to his lymph glands. We tried to plan our wedding as soon as possible, but my father died in May, and we got married in July of 1984.

By this time I had started my real estate career at C.S. Brown Associates and had a bought that brownstone on the Upper West Side. By that fall, Maureen was pregnant. August 8,1985 was one of the greatest days of my life when I held Katharine Alexandra for the first time. She was so beautiful! My only regret was that I had waited so long to have children.

French Lesson Number Twenty-one: *It's never too late.*

Chapter 5

Something Others Want

May 12

One of the first things I ever built was a grocery
store with blocks. Years later, I am still doing it, except the blocks are real.

This week has been uneventful, which is good. I
did run into a friend the other day who asked me how
things were going, and I told him I was writing this
book. I mentioned to him the challenge I have fre-
quently encountered of deciding what to include and
what to exclude. He told me about a dictum he said
was ascribed to Ernest Hemingway, wherein you can
leave *anything* out if—and this is the important part—
if you know you are leaving it out.

"What do you mean?" I asked.

"It's sort of subliminal," he replied. "If you
leave something out because there's something you
don't actually know, the reader will recognize that ig-
norance between the lines, kind of like what happens
in a conversation when a person's uncertainty about a
fact is revealed by his or her tone of voice or the look
in their eyes.

"But if you delete something in a story that you

actually know, that same reader will sense your command of information in the language you use, the way you frame an argument or share a story."

I was pretty sure I followed, but I asked for an example to be certain.

"Imagine," my friend continued, "that you were talking, say, about a ski race, but you didn't mention that one of the racers was injured—because you didn't know. Such an omission would give the lie to your entire report. On the other hand, if you knew that a certain athlete was having financial trouble, your awareness of such a situation would likely color your description of them… even if you left out that the IRS was after them."

I'm not familiar enough with Hemingway or literary theory to debate the thrust of this advice. But the conversation certainly made me think of the need to size up another person, particularly one you are working with or, in my business, about to do a deal with. What is it that they have left out when they say something?

You read the person, and of course they are

reading you, or should be. You're trying to convey a certain persona to them, and they may or may not to you. Some people don't care what they project. They may be so successful in whatever they do that they don't, for want of a better expression, put on airs. Those are actually the kind of people you are more likely to want to work with, versus those who may be trying to create an impression that might be one you don't wish to spend time with.

Meanwhile, and all along, there are these two deal-making phenomena taking place simultaneously. The first, of course, is what brought you and the other party together, as in what was and hopefully still is the impetus for a given deal. I suppose on the one hand that's pretty obvious, but it's easy to forget in instances when the second phenomenon—what's happening at the time in your life, personally or professionally, or both—is pushing or asking for attention.

Every client and every deal is different...yet also there is a commonality. Sometimes that union is less apparent than at others, but sooner or later it will surface for the deal to become real.

FRENCH LESSONS

Real deals…didn't know I was a poet.

The point I was beginning to make is actually profound and had a stunning impact in what became the big break of my career, the one I left you hanging with a few letters ago. To explain, I want to go back again to something else I started to share earlier. The sequence of events that at the time may have seemed almost random was, as I eventually realized, moving me both forward and to a new place.

Recall, if you will, when I had that gallery years ago—it was downtown, by the way, on Mercer Street—and much of the gallery's photo-graphic trove was by the great Berenice Abbott. At one point I con-trolled the duplication of all her work. You were pretty young, Kate, so you may not remember this, but when you were in school a teacher displayed a print of an Abbott photograph, and you told her that your dad had the same one on wall in his office.

"You mean a copy," the teacher corrected you.

"No, the actual photograph," you replied.

And you were right, as you explained to the teacher. You took a picture of the photograph and brought that to school to show her.

But I digress. A year after I began my real estate degree at NYU, I left C.S. Brown Associates and get a job at Brandenburg Realty, a retail brokerage firm in White Plains. It was at NYU that I discovered the world of retail. At the end of the spring semester, in May, it was time for the huge International Council of Shopping Center trade show in Las Vegas, where tenants, owners, and brokers all go to do business. Even though I still had courses to finish, was now the father of two young daughters, and owned investments that were needing my time, I decided to make the trip to Vegas for the trade show.

You can imagine how I must have felt. But sometimes you have to listen to your inner self, even if what it is telling you goes against the grain of common sense.

French Lesson Number Twenty-two: *Follow your intuition.*

Upon my arrival in Las Vegas, one of the first people I met was a man named Walter Minerbi, president of a firm called Landau & Heyman. I told Mr.

Minerbi about my decision to leave office leasing and study at NYU.

"Joe," he said. "There's a property in Yonkers, only a few miles from your home in Bronxville, something of an albatross in our portfolio—a shopping center that is producing no income for us. I'd be happy to let you take a crack at it."

I left the conference very excited over my first exclusive as a retail broker. But after I visited the property, I discovered it was located in the worse part of Yonkers. Plus it was a basically a two-story retail center with a portion of the store fronts facing the Hudson River. I walked up the stairs, stepping over used condoms and crack vials. The business was so bad that soon after my inspection, the owner of a liquor store in the center locked the doors with all his liquor inside and never came back. There was a 400-space parking garage that hardly anyone used, since the few customers of the center walked to the stores and took gypsy cabs home.

Because of my office leasing experience, I was not afraid to make a canvas call to visit retailers. Off I went to a section of Brooklyn with similar stores, where I spoke to the retail tenants. I realized I needed a tenant in Yonkers that would get people to go upstairs. I found a group of furniture stores and made a deal with one of the operators to lease 25,000 square feet. I had an anchor!

Next, I made a deal with a religious school to take a large space facing the river. I agreed that it could use a deck of the parking garage facing the river for a playground. Then I got an optician that accepted Medicare and Medicaid, a Chinese restaurant, and church to lease a store front.

Walter Minerbi was amazed.

"Three other brokerage companies had tried and failed with this center," he told me. Because retail leasing was not very sophisticated at that time, I guessed that the brokers he was referring to probably put signs in windows and hoped someone would show up. Instead of treating this like a traditional grocery-anchored center, I thought outside of the box.

French Lesson Number Twenty-three: *If you want street cred, pound that pavement.*

Now, Landau & Heyman made me the head of leasing for the East Coast—two and a half million square feet of retail space to lease. I was soon responsible for centers that stretched geographically from Albany, New York, to Newport News, Virginia.

~

May 13

Got a little off track there. Mea culpa.

French Lesson Number Twenty-four: *Everything is negotiable if you play your hand from strength.* Let me explain.

With that Yonkers deal, I had not only made a deal but now had a business. The real money in secondary and tertiary centers, I had discovered, was in the small tenants. Anchors of course were important, but they paid a relatively low rent. The important tenants, the ones you had to have to make a shopping center work, were Sally Beauty, a pizzeria, and Subway. And so I became very good at this small-tenant leasing.

Here's how: you start making circles around the

center, driving farther and father out, looking for re-tailers who might be interested in your center. Once you find a prospect, however, you need to know what kind of lease it already has.

I would walk into a store and say I'd like to meet the owner or manager. "How long have you been here?" I'd ask, ever so casually.

Typically, leases in this market are for five or 10 years. So, if someone said he'd been at the location for four years, it was a good guess that he had a lease coming up soon for renewal. That made him a good candidate for relocation at whatever nearby shopping center I was in charge of leasing. If, on the other hand, the person says he's been in his present place for, say, six or seven years, you know he either has extended his five-year lease or is in a ten-year lease. Either way, you make note of this, since you're not in charge of leasing for just one year…you will come back later and visit him again.

Eventually, you tell him who you are and share information about the center you represent. You try to figure out what his rent is and decide what kind of inducements you might offer him, such as cheaper rent or better location. But as you widen that circle around your center, sometimes you get far enough away that you are looking for someone who might consider opening a second store in your center, while keeping his present location.

As I got more deeply into this new experience, an individual whom I had met bought several centers during an economic boom that enabled him to put no money down. As I recall the details, he and his partners—in a firm called Landau & Heyman—owned ten shopping centers with a total value of about 50 million dollars. And that was just one of their portfolios. I ended up leasing another that they owned in the Washington, D.C. area as well as one in Virginia. But the ones that they owned in New York state constituted that group of ten.

The developer of those centers was a company called Big V, a ShopRite affiliate. When they sold the grocery operation to Thomas Lee of Boston, they also sold the real estate to the principals of Landau & Heyman. Big V was able to maximize the value of their operation, giving it the appearance of a sale/leaseback.

McDonald's restaurants is a good example of how a sale/leaseback works. The parent company will buy a piece of land and put up the building that will house the restaurant. Then, McDonald's can make a lot of money by selling the land and paying rent to the new owner for its use. Moreover, McDonald's can get a very aggressive price in the sale because of the company's great credit.

Back to the ten shopping centers: the owners there did basically the same thing, recouping much of their investment through the sale of the property on which the centers were built.

But that wasn't the end of it. The group then went to a savings and loan association and said the value of the centers was going to increase.

"These centers will be worth eighty million once we lease all the space," they argued.

Obviously it wasn't quite as easy as that, but the lenders loaned them the money—fifty millions dollars!

My job, then, was to lease up the space. Once I did that, I became a hero. Leasing agents before this had more or less waited for people to drive and stop when they saw the sign in the window, "For Lease." My feat of finding tenants, using my widening the circle strategy, is what led to the opportunity of leasing spaces in the D.C. and Virginia centers.

French Lesson Number Twenty-five: *Success begets success.*

I remember how in D.C., where they had an office, I would get up in the morning in Bronxville—this was, of course, before 9/11—catch the shuttle, and by 9:30 a.m. be in Washington, where the office was right on the Metro line. So, I could fly into Reagan Airport, hop on the train, and soon I'd be in my Bethesda office. There was a nearby Embassy Suites hotel where I'd stay, but on those Monday morning arrivals I wouldn't even check in. I'd just stop at the hotel, leave my luggage with the concierge, and walk to the office. I'd spend two days there and head back home.

For about a year and a half I followed that routine. To help with the expanding business, I hired a leasing person in the District of Columbia area. He handled the day-to-day in a market that in addition to the city of Washington and suburbs in Virginia soon also included parts of Maryland. And I continued to oversee the centers in the greater New York area. Our clients were tough. The biggest client was Prudential, for which we added a Philadelphia office. Soon there was also a Boston office for centers in Massachusetts.

As I quickly learned, institutional owners were very different from private owners. In the 1990s, a large part of Landau & Heyman's business was third-party management that encompasses leasing. With our help, it was the responsibility of the asset manager to create a budget and project returns for the property. The good news was that the institutions we worked for had acquired great assets. But keeping them leased was a great challenge for us. Asset managers were under great pressure to get good returns for their investors, and it was our responsibility to make them look good.

With asset managers in four different Prudential offices, we knew that each had their own managerial styles. Some managers understood that leasing was not an exact science. Others, who did not, became upset when our projections did not become reality. The difficulty of making those projections turned on trying to predict how many stores would lease and at what rent. Yet, from the day you identified a tenant to the day that tenant moved in, many things could go wrong. There was also the prospect of tenants closing a store because it was underperforming or the retailer was liquidating under a Chapter 7 bankruptcy.

In some such cases, there might have been an over-expansion by the tenant. Or a private equity firm might have bought a retail chain and put too much debt on the business. Ironically, media today often blame such situations on e-commerce, even though e-commerce accounts for only 13 percent of retail shopping. In truth, retailers have come and gone over the years as consumer demands keep constantly changing.

In most of the institutional ownership deals we did, the given institution usually owned the property on which a center was located or on which a center was to be built. Typically, there would be a fund within the institution that was used to buy real estate.

When the inevitable crash came in the in '90s, institutions changed their policy and looked for joint-venture partners who would run the real estate. So, instead of having a third-party manager who had nothing invested in the project, they started having partners who put up, say, ten percent of the equity. In turn, these partners would get fees for managing the property, plus bonuses when the property was especially successful.

I should mention here that leasing stores within centers is time consuming. It's not easy, because everyone's dream—or so it seemed—was to own his or her own business. Perhaps today that is less so than in recent years, as there are fewer so-called mom and pop businesses. Back in the era of my introduction to retail leasing, you might have a Hallmark store or a stand-alone florist. Now supermarkets not only sell Valentine cards, but you can buy the roses there, too. Drugstores sell cards, Walmart sells flowers…forgetting the Internet for a moment, people were
already getting squeezed out of their businesses by the big tenants.

Uh-oh…just realized what time it is. Have a big match at the club today! To be continued.

Much love.

~

Hello again!

Don't ask me about that golf match. Somedays you have it, on this day I did not.

Back to business: my transition to investment sales started with one of the asset managers at Prudential, Dan McNulty, who came to me one day and said he was going to start his own brokerage firm. He wanted to pitch Prudential for the sale of one of its properties that he asset-managed. He and I worked hard on our pitch to the head of disposition in hopes of getting the assignment. We met with Collette Dixon-English, a very accomplished woman of color in a very important role at Prudential who had a reputation for being very tough.

I will always remember coming into the room were Collette was sitting and giving her our pitch book, going through, and answering Collette's questions. Dan and I got the assignment and sold the property at a very good cap rate for the existing market. Dan then went off to start his own very successful company, and I continued to work at Landau & Heyman. This concluded the sale of my first institution property.

We may not have had as many bankruptcies as we have now, but we had similar concerns about how we were going to fill the space. Box tenants were category killers, making it difficult to fill the small store spaces. This changed how centers were built, giving birth to what were called power centers, in which the majority of the center were big box tenants. Today there are fewer buyers of power centers because of the concern about filling the space if you lose a tenant. It is my opinion that if the real estate is good, there are going to be tenants for the space. A great example of is how quickly the former Toys "R" Us spaces are being redeveloped.

The more I think about it, this could be the most important piece of financial advice I share with you.

French Lesson Number Twenty-six: *Know the other person's stakes.*

Come to think of it, this reminds me of another Hemingway story; this one I read online, so I can't vouch for its truth, except to say that if it isn't completely accurate its moral is.

So, there was this man or woman who picked out a dozen or so of the great writer's less famous short stories and retyped them—is that a word we just use in this era of laptops and personal computers? retype?—anyway, made new copies of the stories, with new titles and a fictitious author's name, and put them together into a single manuscript, which was then sent off to several publishers in Boston and New York.

Guess what happened?

Right!

Not a single publisher made an offer, in fact most didn't even reply.

No one, it would appear in this instance, cared about literature. "Is publishing this short story collection by an unknown author going to advance my career?" is clearly the question that must have gone through the minds of the people who received the manuscript.

But, to bring this back to leasing, let us not frame this finally as a negative. It was and remains for me one thing to grasp the other guy's stakes, or lack thereof. But knowing, instead—or, rather, at the same time—what he or she actually *wants* is altogether a different "thing," especially when…strike up the band…when that "thing" is also *something that you have*.

~

June 2

Had to take a call I wasn't expecting, and I wanted to think a bit about this idea of what others want and how it relates—must relate—to what you have. Plus things have been busy at the office as I clear my calendar for the upcoming member guest at the club! And now that it's June, the wedding date in September is suddenly beginning to seem real.

But about having and wanting—put another way, the synchronicity of deal makers, of buyers and sellers, can be defined as a sharing of stakes. This gets complicated, and to begin breaking it down I want to stress that my sense of stakes presumes an expertise or possession. You want to lease retail space, I have such space: I have something you want. Our stakes are complementary. But you also assume here that the space I have is satisfactory, for want of a better word, and I assume as the owner of a business you either have capital or access to such.

This begs for amplification, for the *je ne sais quoi* of those clients I had who'd never actually negotiated a lease. And before I go further I am realizing I ought to add that by the time in my career I was handling those negotiations I was doing so under the umbrella of a company I called…French Associates, which I formally incorporated in 1990, and sold to the Hutensky Group in 1996. By then, it was two years since General Electric had foreclosed on the properties I was working on, only to hire me six months later to lease and then sell the very same properties! Over the next several years, I was in charge of the Hutensky Group's development team that built inner-city shopping centers in which a grocery store was the anchor.

Then, in 2002, I acquired a Sperry Van Ness franchise, and for a decade I managed my own brokerage business. I was in SVN's partner circle as a top ten performer for the company. Finally, in 2012, I sold my franchise—still called French Associates—to Marcus & Millichap, where I am still active as I write these letters.

More about this chronology to come, but enough tooting of my horn for now! Truth is it makes me uncomfortable to talk about myself in this way, but I wouldn't want someone else reading this book to think I was working in corporate isolation all this time. And of course I am proud of what I have accomplished, though that pales in comparison to my feelings about being your father...and, in just a few months, father-in-law of Eliza's husband.

~

June 30

Waylaid once again: the nature of my work...of life. And I had a lot of catching up to do after the annual member-guest tournament at the club. I was playing with a new partner and he seemed a little nervous the first day. By the time over the weekend when we settled into a good rhythm, we were too far behind to catch the leading team in our group.

I could say the following about golf, but let me keep it to business. You know what has always bugged me? People who never get their hands dirty, who live in proverbial ivory towers and deign to tell others what they should do.

CEO's of automobile manufacturers who have never changed the oil in a car.

Airlines executives who don't know the difference between an altimeter and an anemometer.

Leasing agents who have never actually owned something.

When I reflect on my work in retail leasing, especially with its increasing emphasis on institutional clients, I see my early role as part asset manager. We functioned in that role in a third-party sense. Tenants would report to an asset manager, but in the end we actually performed that function. The asset manager would recom-mend, say, that the center needed a new roof, but we were the authority that said yay or nay…we were the decision maker on re-doing a space that had been left a mess by a vacating tenant. Tenants usually leave a space in poor condition, and you don't want people shopping in other stores at the center to look through a window and see trash. It sounds like a little thing, but someone has to remember to cover up those windows! If the tenant that has left was a restaurant, the vacated space is almost always nasty.

By the way, when I just referred to shoppers going from store to store I was referring to their doing so outside, on a sidewalk, in a place where the different businesses abut one another, which is the essence of what people in my business call a shopping center. Colloquially, as of course I know, most folks call this a shopping center. But strictly speaking a mall—a shopping mall—is an enclosed retail space, one where a shopper can go from store to store without having to go back outside.

Despite the short-term popularity of shopping malls, open air centers—another term for shopping centers—tend today to do better than malls. For one thing, rents are generally lower, enabling tenants to price their commodities on a lower scale. In an enclosed mall, a tenant is not only paying rent but also must contribute toward the heating, air conditioning, and upkeep of common space. So, even the landlord's costs are higher. Additionally, when a shopper drives into a shopping center, all the tenants—all the stores— are visible. In a mall, however, you will probably not be able to see all the tenants without parking your car, getting out, and walking into the mall. You might be looking for a store where you can buy new boots, but if you're at a mall you probably can't tell from the outside if there's a shop inside that sells them.

Suppose, though, that you weren't even looking for boots but just out for a drive and while you're tooling around you pass…a mall. But you may not be in the mood for shopping in a huge, overwhelming place that day, so you go on.

Then you pass…a shopping center. Stopped at a red light by the corner, you idly notice a storefront in the center for a shop that sells…boots!

"I've been needing new boots," you remember and…you hang the next left, into the parking lot for the center, and soon you are the owner of…new boots!

Better yet, after you buy the boots you pass a bookstore, also in the center, and…right, it's a new brainer. Stephen King's latest! Maybe even a classic by…Hemingway.

It's all out there in a shopping center. In fact, the best way to build one is to have all the stores facing the highway, where everyone passing by can see what's what. Even if someone is on his or her way to Walmart, that person may see something in the shopping center that prompts them to stop. For the tenants, this means that they may get a customer whom they didn't expect to see at all.

Speaking of things, did you know that Walmart is the number one grocer in the entire world? And that's not the biggest part of their business. Walmart is huge, it's worldwide, an incredibly successful concept.

Not sure why I mentioned that, except that Walmart of course always comes up when you are talking about anchors for shopping centers. Maybe it's the cliched complaint that certain folks make about Walmart's ubiquity and how it's alleged to bully its way into places where people don't want it. You hear a lot of similar complaints about the shopping centers, which for many people—and I mean many, as in millions—are their veritable neighborhoods. Sometimes when I come across a person voicing such an opinion I wonder what he or she thinks about other accoutrements of modern life: the interstate highways on which we drive, the smart phones with which we stay connected.

It's an aphorism to say you can't fight progress. I suppose critics of shopping centers would question their status as progress. And so I ask them: have they grasped the sheer size of this country and the magnitude and needs of its population, the incredible scale of our economy and its infrastructure?

To be continued, my girls!

Chapter 6

All In

August 5

What can I say? Had a couple of short trips and I fell out of my letter-writing routine. Maybe I need to brush up on my own French lessons, lol. This weekend your mother and I are in the Berkshires for a wedding—why does that word make my heart sing?—and I've promised myself to spend some quiet time in this Airbnb where we're staying. It's set quite a bit off the highway in a wooded area. I can hear my muse whispering to me in the wind, reminding me that it's also time to share some reflections on where my peripatetic career was finally taking me, which is also where I still am, deeply grateful to be able to say I'm not only still in the game but also enjoying it more than ever.

So, then, imagine your dad has just been called to the Boston office of an institutional owner whose half-empty shopping center I had just fully leased. Naturally, I am expecting to be congratulated for the great job I had just done, but it turned out that was not the case. Instead...I was fired!

Ironically, as I started to share earlier, I ended up selling my old business to the Hutensky Group, which got my assignment to lease the same property again. Allan Hutensky told me what had happened and how he got the assignment. While playing golf with the chairman of the institution, he had asked for the assignment and because of his relationship he got it. French Lesson Number Twenty-seven: *People want to do business with their friends.*

After this experience, which I will explain in more detail this weekend, I took up golf, which has paid off handsomely for me, professionally and personally. But most of all, I play golf because I love it…in fact, I'm going to sneak off right now to meet a friend at a nearby course just over the Massachusetts/New York border.

Guilty pleasure?

Pleasure, yes…but guilty? No way!

~

August 6

When you come right down to it, leasing a shopping center is a game of chess. Tenants are trying to sneak things into the leases that will cover them in the future, and often landlords miss something or allow it because their focus is on today rather than the impact a decision will have on tomorrow. For example, most grocery store leases exclude gyms from shopping centers. Today, as the retail market continues to change towards more service oriented tenants, gyms are a great tenant to fill vacancy, because they bring people to the plaza.

In some ways, real estate is like a living organism, constantly changing as it ages. I have seen countless tenants come and go. In the 1970s, the advent of VHS players was supposed to usher in the end of movie theaters, but that did not happen. Now we have internet streaming of movies, and once again experts have predicted doom for theaters…yet, as I write this book, I am in the process of doing a new lease for a 35,000 square foot theater so the owner can sell the center!

It is of course clear that there are tenants that are in centers today that will not exist in the future, but a version of this has been going on since the creation of retail. One of the greatest examples is the saga of A&P, the granddaddy of supermarkets, which at one time had nearly 16,000 stores and today does not exist. In my view, the company was either unwilling or unable to change with the times, which is a shame, because as e-commerce continues its present growth, e-commerce retailers are already realizing that they also need brick and mortar stores. When such retailers open stores in a particular market, they typically see as much as a 40 percent increase in sales. Amazon, the leader in e-commerce, has announced it plans eventually to open 3,000 new grocery stores while it also continues to grow the Whole Foods chain it already owns.

My awareness of the reality of change in real estate prepared me for my next act, which was investment sales. As I was about to explain earlier, I merged my business with The Hutensky Group after I was approached by Retail Initiative, a retail fund to develop supermarket anchor centers in underserved markets.

My assignment was to do the leasing for their projects in Harlem and the Bronx. I became Hutensky's head of small store leasing. This included leasing not only a Pathmark grocery in an area of the Bronx that had not a single store but the rest of Hutensky's portfolio of about three million square feet. I had three leasing agents and three support people on my staff, and one of those people still works with me, years later. We were basically third party managers wherein institutions would buy real estate and hire someone to manage and lease the property.

The 1990s were horrible time for real estate investments after the collapse of easy money which lead to over development and change in tax laws. But Brad Hutensky, president of the Hutensky Group, had the foresight to see how the business was changing. Institutional investors in real estate were moving away from third party managers and gravitating toward joint venture partners. Because a joint venture partner has skin in the game, so to speak, it is focused on making the property better in order to earn a promotional bonus tethered to increased value of the center. This development led me to start an investment sales division, which eventually resulted in my selling my way out of a job.

Now I had to decide what to do next. As fate

would have it, I received an email offering me a Sperry Van Ness franchise. The only salary position I had ever had was my six years with the Hutensky Group. It was a very comfortable situation, but the upside was limited. Having your own business does not come without great risk. Two of you daughters were in private school and Kate was about to go to college. After some research, I made a decision to go forward with a plan that I proposed to Brad: I bought the franchise and started my own brokerage business with some help from Brad, who provided me with a nice severance package and my first assignments.

I chose brokerage because it is a business in which I could use the knowledge I had acquired *and* be appropriately compensated. I had worked as part of the development, management team. I had worked on malls, turned malls into traditional shopping centers and made grocery-anchored centers. I had been part of acquisition teams and helped do the underwriting. I had seen what worked and what did not work. I had been involved on many successful projects and some

that were not so successful. I knew I had to place myself within an organization that would provide me with
the support tools need to be successful.

Whew!

My next challenge was to find clients who saw
the value that I could provide. This meant I had to
work harder and smarter than my competition. One of
my first deals was a with a Big Y-anchored center in
East Hartford. I had sold the property to the buyer
while I was at the Hutensky Group. It was a difficult
sale, because Big Y had less than two years on the
lease. The seller initially thought it needed a big name
brokerage company to make the sale. After six months
of no offers, the owners decided to give me a chance. I
told them that we needed to market the property at a
price that made it look like a deal, but one in which
they would still make a profit.

Unfortunately, Cushman & Wakefield were
used to marketing class A properties to a small group
of buyers. We called these properties the low hanging
fruit. I knew I was going to have to expand the buyer

group beyond their typical buyer. I turned to international markets, generat-ing calls and offers from Israel—all of which, alas, my seller turned down. I finally got a promoter who offered a price acceptable to my seller.

But there was a problem: the buyer was trying to flip the contract and so it kept asking for extensions. The seller gave the extensions with my advice to request that money be released from escrow to the seller. Normally, the money would become nonrefundable but would be kept in the escrow account, giving the buyer opportunity to sue for his refund. That would essentially freeze the money in the account, with the hope that the seller would end the lawsuit with at least a partial refund even if there was a default, per the contract.

After a number of extensions, the seller had been paid a million dollars, and so we told the buyer there would be no more extensions. The buyer had no choice but to close, or else it would lose the million dollars. The buyer then bought its first and last shopping center. The seller has since given me many more millions of dollars in real estate to sell.

One very smart client bought a deal for 13 million dollars and then with improvements and sold the property with a profit of 16 million. At the age of 42, he retired to Florida, where he built an 8,000 square foot house that includes a portion he calls the French wing!

~

August 7

This will probably be my last letter before the wedding. We're still in the Berkshires, and I'd like to go back to something I elided over yesterday.

After leaving the Hutensky Group to start my own business with the purchase of a Sperry Van Ness franchise, I soon transitioned from retail leasing to investment sales. But, as I meant to explain earlier, initially I did both. The moment that finalized my transition was the leasing of a property I sold in the Bronx for a million dollars and then, after much negotiation, ground-leased half of the property to a tenant for 49 years. The lawyer for the owner and I spent so much time together that we became best of friends, playing golf and sharing social occasions with our wives and children. As we met with the tenant and their lawyers, and the owner and his lawyer, to sign the lease, the owner leaned over to me to say what a great job I had done.

Hmmm.

Sure enough, he then announced that he could not then pay me my commission. Instead, he said he would pay me over the course of the lease, as the tenant paid him.

As I realized, the problem with leasing is you create great value for the landlord, but there is no immediate compensation for the owner. This require the landlord to come out of pocket to pay your commission. When I worked for institutional owners this was never a problem, but when you work for family office or individuals they are never quick to pay you the commission for a deal of some size.

In this case, I had increased the value by a factor of four times what the owner had paid for the property with a ground lease. This meant that the owner did not have to spend a dime to put the tenant in place, as the tenant built out their own space. And the deal was for only half of the property, producing cash flow that would allow him to live comfortably for the rest of his life.

Investment sales, as I could see, required as much work as retail, but at the conclusion of investment work I would be paid at closing.

Voila!

I now needed to develop this business, again with the assistance of Brad Hutensky, who gave me a number of properties to market. I was off to the races! The challenge for me was to prove that I could do a better job than the brokers at the so-called Big Three: Cushman & Wakefield, CBRE, and JLL.

I knew this was going to be an uphill battle. The Big Three were perceived as the best because they were the biggest. But the big money for these companies was in office leasing rather than investment sales. Their investment sales business was initially the sale of institutional properties. These properties were in high demand and the pool of buyers was small. I had one institutional owner tell me he always used one of the Big Four because no one would ever question his decision if the sale failed. These brokers all knew the small group of buyers and would of course reach them easily.

It took some thought, but I saw that this reality actually presented opportunities for me. When one of the Big Three took on assignments, there was no sense among their small group of buyers that their sales would fail. One such deal was for the sale of a grocery anchor center in East Hartford. The grocer Big Y had a year left on its lease. You may remember I had not only leased the center, but had sold the center to the group they had chosen—Cushman & Wakefield—to sell its as they thought this would get them the most money. After their lack of success, they then reached out to me.

This was not an easy assignment, but I knew I was not just going to reach out just to the usual buyers. I needed someone who would be more focused on yield than on simply understanding how the center worked. I started looking at foreign buyers that would focus on yield. I was able to identify potential buyers in Israel and investors in the Orthodox community and create a bidding situation. As I mentioned before, I was then able to get a large nonrefundable deposit and have the buyer close at price greater than what Cushman & Wakefield had projected (and by the way had not gotten offers anywhere near the sale price).

To replicate this with a shopping center in Roosevelt Field, Long Island was my next success. That location was one of the hottest retail areas in the New York metropolitan market. But the property had several problems. It was an old warehouse building that had converted to retail and sold to First Allied, which had then been sold to the present owner. Every time it sold, the seller had made money and the market was not as hot when this present group had bought the property. The property had problems, including insufficient parking. Also, it was a converted warehouse, where the stores were somewhat hidden and hard to lease. And it had a securitized mortgage, which could not be paid off without being assessed a large penalty. This meant you needed to find someone willing to assume the loan putting a down payment of over 40 per cent.

With Eastdil secured producing no offers, the sellers then reached out to me. We were able to generate lots of interest, but we were not getting buyers that were either willing to pay the price or willing to make a large down payment. We opened up the property to the brokerage community, something the large firms claim they do but they don't. What they more typically do is say to the broker that he can bring a buyer, but the buyer has to pay the buy-side broker. This puts the buyer at a disadvantage, because it is now paying two brokerage fees.

We offered to split our fee to make sure we got the highest price the market would pay. Next, a broker new to the market had a multi-tenant owner that he had met at his temple and who was in need of a 1031 exchange—a strategy that allows an investor to "defer" paying capital gains taxes on an investment property when it is sold, as long as another "like-kind property" is purchased with the profit gained by the sale of the first property. His buyer had a 15 million-dollar gain, the property was perfect for him, and the sale was concluded!

~

What a glorious time that was in Italy! Perfect weather, with the temperature in the 70s. I can still see in my mind's eye that blue sky at the countess's mansion in Fiesole, up on the hills overlooking Florence. Eliza, as I recalled in my wedding toast, I remember the earlier, Cape Cod wedding we attended together and the moment afterwards when I looked up toward the heavens and said, of your now dearly betrothed, "God, let him be the one!"

Now, weeks later, as I happily adjust to the realization that I have a son-in-law, it's something of a challenge to be back at the office. Not to compare, but in the spirit of your nuptials, I would like to share how to close a deal by being all in. Jeff Stearney and I were working on a property that I had received from a long-term client. It was a property with which we were able to generate a lot of interest. But the owner had an over-protective lawyer, and so we went through two buyers who we were unable sign a contract. This wasted over four months, with basically nothing accomplished.

The next time we found a buyer, we shared the contract and told the buyer what points were non-negotiable. This third attempt ended with a signed contract!

The buyer was very diligent and did a comprehensive review of the property. Unfortunately, our client—the owner—had to be taken to a hospital because he was suffering from an antibiotic-resistant infection. This happened before the deal was completed. Our client was very sick and in a great deal of pain.

At the same time, the buyer re-traded by asking for almost a million dollar price reduction. Our immediate response was that you need to sharpen your pencil, because this reduction is a nonstarter. The buyer came back with a $300,000 re-trade. The price now fell between the low and the high that we had given the seller. The contract price was higher by $200,000.

Jeff—one of the talented men in the group I oversee—went to the hospital, where he had to put on an infectious disease gown before he could meet with the seller. Shortly after his arrival, the seller experienced a "code red" medical event and nearly died. Nevertheless, Jeff was able to discuss the contract issue with the seller, who reluctantly agreed to a $50,000 price reduction.

Meanwhile, the buyer told us that he was at the highest price he was willing to pay. That left us still a quarter of a million dollars apart. We knew that the buyer had been working on this deal for over four months and had close to six figures already invested in the deal.

We were now communicating with the seller's other partner, who would not make any decisions without the other partner's approval. We shared this with the buyer, who then increased his offer, leaving us now only $125,000 apart.

A few days later, the buyer informed us that he would be sending a termination letter that would into effect in 24 hours.

Two hours before the deadline, the seller's partner again refused to reduce the price. The buyer said he would not negotiate further. Jeff and I quickly reviewed the overall deal and saw that it was in the best interest of the seller to counter because the property loan was coming due. The buyer was prepared to close before that date. We were also at a price that was now north of our opinion of value.

Armed with these reasons for why the seller should sell, Jeff drove back to the hospital, again donned infectious disease gear, and met once more with the seller, who still refused to reduce his price, splits the difference with the buyer, or have the broker and the seller split the difference with the buyer.

With 15 minutes remaining to get the deal done, the buyer agreed to increase his price by $75,000 and the Seller agreed to reduce the price by $63,000…and we as the broker made up the difference!

That's being all in, a career-defining French Lesson (number 28): *Be all in, whatever you do.*

~

Thanksgiving

I was up early today, like I usually am, and it was such a lovely morning for late November that I took my protein shake with me and sat out back on the patio, reflecting on the ebb and flow of life, of giving and receiving.

I prefer the term charity to giving back. To me, the term giving back implies that you have borrowed or stolen something and now are returning it. Whereas charity, defined by Immanuel Kant, is "to make good on past injustices."

My dear daughters, your lives have been rich in accomplishment and happiness, and the fact that we have the ability to make good on past injustices is our duty to fellow mankind. In my own life, I have been fortunate to have chosen to do things where I have actually been able to see the difference I have made.

I have been fortunate to be able to do this with the support of my friends at a golf tournament I have chaired for 18 years. The support of my church in raising funds and building homes has also been significant. I have been overcome when meeting the children of families we helped, who have now grown up, gone to college, and started families of their own. They are shining examples of breaking the cycle of poverty.

FRENCH LESSONS

Another activity that I have supported and you have had a chance to witness and support is Crossing Thresholds, an organization that works directly with the people it helps, learning from them and building schools with them. In the largest slum in Africa, which is also the second largest slum in the world, one and a half million people live in an area the size of Central Park. I know you remember when I had the opportunity to take all three of you to this place, which is called Kibera. There, Crossing Thresholds found a women teaching kids in a dirt lot but today there is a school in place which feeds, clothes, and educates 300 students.

Chloe, I am so grateful and proud that your experience in Kibera was a catalyst for your public health major in college and beyond. Today, with a gifts of dollar a day per child, Crossing Thresholds supports four schools, ranging from daycare to high school, with over a 1,000 students. Some of the graduates are in college and will soon have a college education, something that their parents never had a chance to achieve. Once again, the cycle of poverty is broken.

FRENCH LESSONS

Working in Kibera was something I will never forget. The poverty there was unbelievable. Families lived in mud and stick building covers with a sheet of corrugated metal. There was no clean water, electricity or any public utilities. A river running through Kiberia was basically a sewer. Before schools built a dormitory for girls, they were in constant danger of being raped.

Through the Reformed Church of Bronxville, I have been involved for the last 30 years in the Mission Council. Our latest program, Coming Home, was created by our mission director, Dawn Ravella. This is an 18- week program that helps formerly incarcerated men and women transition to society. The success of the program has led to creation of other coming home programs at other churches.

To be involved with Coming Home was a chance to support people who are released from prison with neither a job nor a place to live. This program provide mentors which now support in helping them get adjusted to society.

I am so proud that one of you—Katharine—is a graduate of its Real Estate Associate Program (REAP), an industry-backed , market–driven program that serves as a bridge between talented minority professionals and commercial real estate companies looking for talent. The program has seen it graduates go to work at such firms as MacDonald's, IKEA, and Newmark Knight Frank.

REAP is dear to my heart, because it enables me to help smart, well educated young people discover the world of real estate. I have often heard from human resources professional that they would hire minority if they could only find them. REAP helps them find them.

All of these programs have something in common in that for me it was not just a board position but an opportunity to be involved with changing people's lives, "making good on pass injustices."

Of course, none of this would be possible for me had I not learned through many lessons to be the best investment sales broker that I could be. Having closed many deals that larger firms had tried and failed, I have learned to listen to buyers and sellers and enable them to achieve their goals. In the many years that I have been doing investment sales, I have also learned that no deal is the same as another. Markets are constantly changing and you are dealing with companies whose goals maybe are to make money, but how they are going to achieve this is always evolving.

There are people who have the vision and luck to predict were the market is going and they hit financial home runs. In today's market, for example, it can seems like the news is a constant series of failing retailers. Many institutions and private investors are running from retail properties while others re realizing that great returns can be achieved with minimum risk.

I still get up everyday looking forward to going to battle with the intension of winning. I do not get all the assignments that I think I deserve even when I know that my team and I are the best team to get it done, to achieve the highest price the market will pay. I have had many doors shut in front of me and I been told I am not good enough, but my early experiences have taught me that you need to keep fighting and show them that they are wrong. So don't be a quitter and you will succeed, or as my mother used to remind me—French Lesson Number Twenty-nine: *Be the best you can be.*

Afterword and Acknowledgments

First, I would like to thank my team: Jodi Tomany, Tom Dalzell, Jeff Stearney, Roger Ready, Schuyler Boylan and Brad Thomas—without their help I would not be here. John Kruger, thank you for all your support. J.D, unfortunately I have come to have a big regret about Marcus & Millichap, which is that I should have joined Marcus & Millichap years ago. Thank you for your continued support.

I want to give a special thanks to composer and pianist Nils Vigeland and Maddy Burke-Vigeland, an architect, whose introduction to writer Carl Vigeland helped make this book happen. I am also grateful to Nils and Maddy for their careful reading of an early draft. They are the definition of great friends.

It is important to acknowledge Carter Via, who introduced me to volunteering for charity. I first met him at the Reformed Church nursery school that one of my daughters was attending. A minster at the church, he was the school's chaplain. One day he was in my den and we were discussing the ills of the world and somehow we got on the conversation that I needed to do something to make the world a little better place to live. The next thing I knew, I was on the board of Habitat in Yonkers. After leaving the church, Carter went on to start Bridges to Community, a Nicaraguan organization that provides international trips for volunteers of development projects that meet real needs. I lost track of Carter during that period, but one day I ran into him again on a golf course and he told me about Crossing Thresholds. Soon I was on a plane to Africa with two of my daughters.

~

Beth Shepard a childhood friend who with her mother Carol Ruth opened my eyes to photography through their Photograph Workshop, through which I developed a lasting love of photography, which in turn led to the opportunity to meet great artist such as Paul Caponigro, George Tice, Ansel Adams , and Wynn Bullock, among others. I remember sitting in Yosemite Valley in Ansel Adam's home, looking at photographs and learning about what he called zone theory. I remember asking Ansel how he slept at night when he sold photographs for $250 each, while everyone else in the room sold theirs for $100 or less. Fortunately, I bought a couple, and I later sold one for $65,000.

I had the opportunity to be on the ground floor of an art market that went from values that barely supported the artist to making s and dealers millionaires. This led me to meet and represent Berenice Abbott. Through my relationship with Berenice, I had one of the greatest nights of my life. Berenice was being honored by International Center of Photography at Top of the World restaurant in the twin towers. The event was chaired by Jackie Kennedy Onassis. I will always remember walking into the room and having Berenice wave me over to meet her new friends, one of whom was Jackie O. During our conversation, I realized they both suffered from vertigo and could not look out the windows at the incredible view. They stood with their backs to the windows. The room was full of other celebrities and business elites, and they all wanted to talk to me and my artist. A young man from meager means had arrived.

~

Later, I met a young woman who introduced me to her boss, Rick Rogers, an agent at CAA. Rick had moved from Los Angeles, California, to Westport, Connecticut, and knew nobody in town. We became friends. His job required him to attend a concert every night, where he met a mix of established and new artists. He suggested that I could be a promoter. The next thing I knew, I had leased the Capitol Theatre in Port Chester, New York. Our landlord was Phillip Steinberg, who was a character from a B. movie. He made sure we saw that he had a nickel-plated, pearl-handled, .25-caliber handgun. He drove a 1970 white Eldorado Cadillac and dressed very flamboyantly. We signed the lease without any legal representation, and I am sure if we had failed to make our payments we would have lost what little we had of any future earnings we might make.

The theater had been made famous by Howard Stein, who brought in such bands as Joe Cocker, Pink Floyd, and Janis Joplin. It was a tough business, with many challenges. One of the artists I represented was John Mayall, who was to perform two shows. Someone told me about a friend that had a pink limo with a female chauffeur. I hired them and got CBS News to cover Mayall's arrival for local news story. I went to LaGuardia Airport to meet him. As he deplanes, a ten-year-old limo arrived and out pops a young black man from the passenger side who is dressed like a pimp. On the driver's side, a young women got out. She was wearing hot pants, a chauffeur's hat, and a leather vest for a top, all in pink.

More than three hours later, my partner and I were still waiting at the theater for the limo's arrival. The backup band and the sound crew had completed sound check and a quick rehearsal. At 6:30, we got a call from the driver, asking how far the theater was from Newark NJ was. They were at least a hour away. We had 1,800 people waiting come into the theater with a second show at 10:00. My partner and I decided to consult with security and decided to tell the crowd that the first show was cancelled and that we would offer a credit for a future show. It was my job to give the crowd the bad news. Another lesson learned.

It was quite an experience, during an era for artists when drugs and booze was big. And the artist was guaranteed a price that allowed the promoter to make about ten percent of revenue if the theater sold out. The promoter took all the risk with only a small upside. I soon decided there was far better future in fine art photography.

~

Special thanks to Scott Brown for giving me a chance to succeed in a business he told me was racist I learned a lot at C.S. Brown Associates, and we had fun getting it done. It was incredibly boring work making cold calls, but when you got an assignment it was challenging and fun working with titans of New York City during a time when people worked and played hard. Two- Martini lunches were no longer fully tax-deductible, but that did not stop clients from expecting it. One of my favorite memories of working at C.S. Brown is the time after my dog had died and I had the ashes shipped to the office. The package arrived, and the young women brought it back to my cubicle and asked what it is.

"It is my dog," I said.

She turned the box around several times.

"How does it breathe?" she asked.

David Itzkowitz, my cubicle buddy, taught me the business. I even learned how to spell his name backwards and forwards. And I learned how to make a cold call and not to get depressed when people hung up on us. I have enjoyed his friendship as we have watched our children grow up and set out into the world. I was able take what I learned and convert the knowledge to my work in retail leasing.

The late Peter Brandenberg hired me even though he also told me that the real estate business was racist and I would not succeed. This was the continuation of a theme I chose not to embrace. Peter convinced me to go to Las Vegas for the ICSC convention, even though I did not have adequate income and the trip cost several thousands dollars. And he introduced me to the man who changed my life.

~

Walter Minerbi gave me the chance of a life time with my first exclusive to lease a shopping center in the depressed section of Yonkers. With his help, I was responsible for a couple million square feet of space.

Brad Hutensky taught me to make sure you treat everyone with respect in hopes that they will do the same to you. He underwrote the cost of getting my CCIM, enabling me to become a much better investment sales broker. He allowed me to start an investment sales division, which meant I had a deadly combination for underwriting deals, both from a financial standpoint and an understanding of how the shopping center worked. Brad and his father Allan taught me the love of golf, introducing me to the game at their club. I also join Allen for poker nights at his clubs in Connecticut or Florida. When I left their company I was better prepared for the next stage of my life.

I want to thank Rob Levin for sending me the email that offered the Sperry Van Ness franchise, which allowed me to polish my investment sales skill by working with some of the country's most successful brokers. I want to thank Mark Van Ness, Rand Sperry, and David Frosh for creating such a great company, including its Partner Circle, which celebrates our achievements. One of the highlights of my professional life was making the circle's top ten and speaking at The Beverly Hills Hilton in Beverly Hills CA before a crowd of more than on thousand people. I was especially proud because one of my daughters was in the audience.

Finally, I want to thank J.D. Parker for convincing me to join Marcus & Millichap, which has given me an opportunity to take my business to another level.

~

As I come to the end of this book, these acknowledgments remind me of a final French Lesson (number thirty): *Give thanks for blessings large and small.*

As I said at the beginning—and say to myself each day—none in my life could be larger than you three and the mother who brought each of you into a world made richer and happier for all who know you.

Appendix

French Lessons

1. You make your own life.

2. Judge not by appearances.

3. You cannot change what is done, but you can make your future.

4. By your presence will you be known.

5. Know thy neighbor.

6. Do what you have to do.

7. Create and you will be rewarded.

8. When something's not working, fix it.

9. Never rush unless you have to.

10. Know who you are.

11. Look first, but then remember to leap.

12. First impressions are important.

13. Knowledge is key.

14. Learn from life's detours.

15. Stop, look, and if it looks good, chance it.

16. Never talk in an elevator.

17. Treat everyone the same.

18. Be prepared.

19. Listen to the person with the primary interest.

20. Take care of the person with the primary interest.

FRENCH LESSONS

21. It's never too late.

22. Follow your intuition.

23. If you want street cred, pound that pavement.

24. Everything is negotiable if you play your hand from strength.

25. Success begets success.

26. Know the other person's stakes.

27. People want to do business with their friends.

28. Be all in, whatever you do.

29. Be the best you can be.

30. Give thanks for blessings large and small.

Made in USA - Kendallville, IN
1198299_9780578649948
11.21.2020 0842